MW00638343

ALSO BY BEN LERNER

THE LIGHTS

THE LIGHTS

Poems

BEN LERNER

FARRAR, STRAUS AND GIROUX
NEW YORK

Farrar, Straus and Giroux
120 Broadway, New York 10271

Copyright © 2023 by Ben Lerner
All rights reserved
Printed in the United States of America
First edition, 2023

Library of Congress Cataloging-in-Publication Data
Names: Lerner, Ben, 1979– author.
Title: The lights : poems / Ben Lerner.
Description: First edition. | New York : Farrar, Straus and Giroux, 2023.
Identifiers: LCCN 2023008688 | ISBN 9780374279219 (hardcover)
Subjects: LCGFT: Poetry.
Classification: LCC PS3612.E68 L54 2023 | DDC 811/.6—dc23/eng/20230306
LC record available at https://lccn.loc.gov/2023008688

Designed by Gretchen Achilles

Our books may be purchased in bulk for promotional, educational, or business
use. Please contact your local bookseller or the Macmillan Corporate and
Premium Sales Department at 1-800-221-7945, extension 5442, or by email at
MacmillanSpecialMarkets@macmillan.com.

www.fsgbooks.com
www.twitter.com/fsgbooks • www.facebook.com/fsgbooks

10 9 8 7 6 5 4 3 2 1

for Lucía, for Marcela

CONTENTS

THE LIGHTS

INDEX OF THEMES

Poems about night
and related poems. Paintings
          about night,
sleep, death, and
                    the stars.
I know one poem from
school under the stars, but
belong to no school
          of poetry.
I forgot it by heart. I remember only
it was set in the world and its theme
          parted.

          Poems
about stars and
how they are erased by street
lights,
          streets
in a poem about force
and the schools within it. We learned
all about night in college,
          how it applies,
night college under the stars where we
          made love
a subject. I completed my study of form

          and forgot it.
Tonight,
          poems about summer

and the stars are sorted by era
over me.

        Also poems about grief
and dance. I thought I'd come to you
with these themes
        like my senses.
Do you remember me
from the world?
        I was set there and we spoke

on the green, likening something
        to prison, something
to film.
        Poems about dreams
like moths about streetlights
until the clichés
        glow, soft
glow of the screen
comes off on our hands,
        blue prints on the windows.
How pretentious
        to be alive now,

        let alone again
like poetry and poems
        indexed by
cadences falling about us while
parting. It was important to part
yesterday

        in a serial work about lights
so that distance could enter the voice
and address you
        tonight.
Poems about you, prose
        poems.

THE STONE

Imagine a song, she said, that gives voice to people's anger. These weren't her actual words. The anger precedes the song, she continued, but the song precedes the people, the people are back-formed from their singing, which socializes feeling, expands the domain of the feelable. The voice must be sung into existence, so song precedes speech, clears the ground for it. Then how are we speaking now, I asked, although not in those words. We aren't, she responded. Or we are, but only about whether one should take her cat to the vet in a pandemic, if I should form a pod with my neighbors, if mangoes are stone fruit. A people's voice isn't speaking through us. I pulled a handful of grass from the earth, which left the earth with almost no resistance. We're just talking, she continued, which isn't really speaking; talk precedes the song that makes speech possible. But we can talk about singing, we can describe the song and its conditions, sitting on our blankets in Fort Greene Park, the taped-off police cruiser still smoldering nearby, dragonflies mating aloft in the humid air above us. Can the song be talked into existence, I asked, I wanted to ask, just as I wanted the grass to resist more, to cling more passionately to the earth. The stems are hollow except at the nodes. They have evolved to withstand trampling and storms. I bequeath myself to the dirt to grow from the grass I love, the poet wrote, which is neither speech nor singing, but a grassy area between them, cordoned off by cops. (Strange how "poet" and "cop" are anagrams.) Agitated starlings had gathered in the trees. Let's think up some new collective nouns, she didn't say. An agitation of starlings. A bevy, a herd, a game, a flight, a pod, a murder of people with stone voices, pinned to the ground of experience, the ethical ground. In that sense throwing stones is close

'hen you shatter glass, which is made by heating grass into

1 the goal of song is to liquify things, the singer most of

all. When she sings, she can't pull the song back out, and when she flees, she leaves behind parts of her digestive tract, muscles, nerves; you can hear that sorrowful foreknowledge in the song. Smoke masks pheromones so the keeper can access the hive (strange that "song" and "smoke" are homophones), but even a dead singer can sing, even a singer a scrub jay has decapitated will sing if you step on it.

AUTO-TUNE

1

The phase vocoder bends the pitch of my voice toward a norm.

Our ability to correct sung pitches was the unintended result of an
    effort to extract hydrocarbons from the earth:

the technology was first developed by an engineer at Exxon to
    interpret seismic data.

The first poet in English whose name is known learned the art of
    song in a dream.

Bede says: "By his verse the minds of many were often excited to
    despise the world."

When you resynthesize the frequency domain of a voice, there is
    audible "phase smearing," a kind of vibrato,

but instead of signifying the grain of a particular performance, the
    smear

signifies the recuperation of particularity by the normative.

I want to sing of the seismic activity deep in the earth and the
    destruction of the earth for profit

in a voice whose particularity has been extracted by machine.

I want the recuperation of my voice, a rescaling of its frequency
    domain, to be audible when I'm called upon to sing.

2

Caedmon didn't know any songs, so he withdrew from the others in
   embarrassment.
Then he had a dream in which he was approached,
probably by a god, and asked to sing "the beginning of created
   things."
His withdrawing, not the hymn that he composed in the dream, is
   the founding moment of English poetry.
Here my tone is bending toward an authority I don't claim
   ("founding moment"),
but the voice itself is a created thing, and corporate;
the larynx operates within socially determined parameters we learn
   to modulate.
You cannot withdraw and sing, at least not intelligibly.
You can only sing in a corporate voice of corporate things.

3

The voice, notable only for its interchangeability, describes
the brightest object in the sky after the sun, claims
love will be made beneath it, a voice leveled to the point that I can
    think of it as mine.
But because this voice does not modulate the boundaries of its
    intelligibility dynamically, it is meaningless.
I can think of it as mine, but I cannot use it to express anything.
The deskilling of the singer makes the song transpersonal at the
    expense of content.
In this sense the music is popular.

Most engineers aspire to conceal the corrective activity of the phase
    vocoder.
If the process is not concealed, if it's overused, an unnatural warble
    in the voice results,
and correction passes into distortion: the voice no longer sounds
    human.
But the sound of a computer's voice is moving, as if our technology
    wanted to remind us of our power,
to sing "the beginning of created things." This is the sound of our
    collective alienation,
and in that sense is corporate. As if from emotion,

the phase smears as the voice describes
the diffuse reflection of the sun at night.

4

In a voice without portamento, a voice in which the human
is felt as a loss, I want to sing the permanent wars of profit.
I don't know any songs, but won't withdraw. I am dreaming
the pathetic dream of a pathos capable of redescription,
so that corporate personhood becomes more than legal fiction.
A dream in prose of poetry, a long dream of waking.

Slow-moving objects flying in groups
Lights in the trees. Like those minutes before
the storm when we stood at Kyle's wedding
looking up. A decision has to be made
about taking shelter. Too high to be birds
too slow to be conventional aircraft
her white dress stood out against the dark gray
sudden drop in pressure. Lights
in the trees. Slow-moving. The radar
we shut the radar down and recalibrated to rule out ghost tracks

No notable exhaust from a known propulsion system in other words
I want to know what it would do
to the art if they are not Russian
What I mean by "erratic" is
unknown sources. A beautiful ceremony
because the wall cloud visible behind them
has to be made. I was in Paris once
with Bobby who was mourning his mother
and filming public sculptures. Every few hours he would
in tears. And I would hold him. It is rare for me

to hold a male friend, but I was and looked up to see
these lights. Now, my degree is not in physics
so it is important I rise early and try to get it all down
before my echo. Like walking to meet
Mónica I must have got too much sun
sat on the curb suddenly cold and looked up
to the art. The video shows a source of heat

Birds are out of the question. I have learned to hold
the back of the head when we embrace, it adds
a sense and also slows it down like

if they do make contact and the dead missed it
my mom missed it, he said, a break
in all human understanding she wasn't here for and I
was like: One, they might have ways
of ministering to the dead and two
and two, there are deep resources in the culture for trying to
understand. The sightlines
of the sculptures he was filming
had these moths in them. No way a human pilot could
unless the outer shell was a cavity filled with gas

2

At least the white poets might be trying to escape, using
the interplanetary to scale
down difference under the sign of encounter and
late in a way of thinking, risk budgets
the steal, the debates about face
coverings, deepfakes, we would scan
the heavens, discover what we've projected there
among the drones, weather events, secret programs
I'm no doubt doing some of that when
I hold the back of his head and see
unexplained lights over him
that love makes, even if what I want in part
is to be destroyed, all of us
at once, and so the end of desire is caught in it

I think it is ok to want that, that wrong desire
must have its place in your art, that the trails
ice probably, and we are alone
and we are not alone with being
Out for the first time since the pandemic, we fought
about the dog and who is allowed to use the word
"Palestine," and then almost made up about how
the insolubility, how every problem
scales, and I made my joke
which is not a joke, about the leaked footage
our only hope. Is the work
to get outside the logic of solution or to work
as if there were one, ones

among us. I'm sure they are almost all military
but when the neighbor cut my hair
she was masked, we were outside, she told me her
cousin had been abducted and treated very gently
that they have to make contact somehow
they are waiting for us to evolve
gray hair on the pavement among the cherry
blossoms. And I said
I want to be honest with you, yes, you do sound crazy
I want to believe your story because there is love
in it. Once I was in Paris and my
friend's mom was in the trees
he didn't see, I had to hold him and that knowledge

3

that they are here
among us, that they love us
that we invited them
in without our knowledge
into our knowledge, its cavities
that we have asked to be destroyed
that they are deliberating
in us, that they are part of our sexual life
that they are baffled by us, gentle
to our cousins

that they take the form
that forms can be taken up
that the form is reflected in the Seine
the rim of the glass at Kyle's wedding
that they are patient
to the point of nonexistence
that they can withstand forces no human pilot
that they have arts
that they are known to our pets
that if you put a pet down

they are beside it without judgment
that they smell vaguely of burning paper
that to meet them would be to remember meeting them
as children, that they are
children, that the work of children is
in us, that they are part of our sexual life
that they are reading this

that they are baffled but can make out
the shape of a feeling to which they assign
no number, gender

that they have sources
of lift

At some point I realized the questions were the same questions. I'm studying implicit race bias in toddlers. I'm tracking the advent of the credit economy. The implications for folk music of the fact that stars don't twinkle—the apparent perturbation of stars is just a fluctuation in the medium—is something we want to understand. We want to understand the way it changes our memories of bedtime, for instance. A green flash. Twinkle twinkle. That's funny, a man in the atrium says, I'm studying the same question. In different terms. I'm living out that question as kindly as possible; in fact, that's why I'm here today volunteering. You have to admit, the staff is doing an excellent job. Then he sips his tea in a paper cup. Then he describes an experience of defibrillation. The other day I went to see the realignment of a permanent collection; abstraction had been demoted. I had complicated thoughts about it, which I carried into the winter sun, where I realized: That's the same question, pressing my face into her inner thigh. Calling a friend in agony. For folk music, the implications are profound. Rhythm shapes feeling. That way abstraction can rise again, rinsed of dominance, a blue rinse for the tradition, little star. Only then is it possible to pose the question, cup the question, blow on it gently. Is recumbency necessary to facilitate analytic revelry. Is your mom really capable of hearing you, given her level of anxiety. To use an example from my own life, I sleep with my head under the pillow. I think it's pretty common for men my age. But do we have a sufficient account of those rhythms of behavior as they spread out across a generation. Now a purpose for the arts comes into focus, leaving a bright halo around the body. The way psychoanalysis lacks an account of nut milks. How the term "labor" plays about the lips of humanists. I develop predictive technologies for complex scenarios. I slow down popular songs and play them over footage of sunflowers tracking east. That's funny, a man says. When I was a kid I thought all the skyscrapers were department stores, imagined the top floors were devoted to toys, and when the towers came down I kept imagining large stuffed animals in a panic, a few leaping to their deaths. The moon is not the sun at night. How I wonder what you are. Many stones contain small amounts of poison and the nectarine is no exception. These are things I've never said out loud before, how much his personality depends upon holding a hot drink, a small continuous exhibition of care that contrasts with the viciousness of his speech. Wool has more body than rayon. Or does the tape say "viscousness," syntax behaving like a solid, providing light and ventilation. As a blue flame spreads across a shallow liquid spill, I'm trying to imagine a lullaby that scales. I was taught this printing method in a dream. It contains a hidden countermelody. All I remember from your course, she told me, is that the rose is obsolete. We'd run into each other on the Queens-bound G, and I couldn't figure out if I should ask her about the bruising on her neck and face. We emerged out of the tunnel into winter sun and around her body a bright halo formed. Can I ask you a personal question. Have you ever felt like your speech is being dictated by phonological associations to such a degree that even—or maybe especially—in your most intimate relationships, the content of your utterances is driven by the demands of acoustical shape. This troubles inwardness. This opens onto the problems of consent. Auditory memory traces are subject to rapid decay, like a diamond in the sky. Rose was my maternal grandmother's name. Her parents had a small grocery store in Brooklyn. They hired a driver for deliveries who came highly recommended. But—as they learned only after he struck and killed a pedestrian—he had no license. They were sued and lost everything. My great-grandfather went more or less insane.

He also suffered from boils. My great-grandmother died from tuberculosis in a sanatorium with concrete floors. Neither spoke English. Rose had to raise her younger brother John in poverty, more or less alone. Many years later, John—who by this point was a pioneering anthologist of folk music—was hit and killed by a Hasidic Jew hurrying home for the Sabbath. Late in Rose's life, these two car accidents became confused in her mind. Her father had hired a Hasidic Jew who struck and killed her baby brother. But that's not why I'm telling you this story, she said. When Rose was in an assisted-living home in Cambridge, she became convinced that the staff were sneaking into her room and subtly altering her paintings. Taking the canvases out of the frames, adding another outline around the apples and pears, restoring the paintings to their places. My cousin would always argue with her: Are you crazy, who would do such a thing, nobody is touching your paintings. This went on for around a year. Until one day my dad—we were all in town for her ninetieth birthday—got up from his chair, walked to the wall, removed his glasses, inspected the artworks carefully, and said: Well, Rose, you are the one who really knows these paintings. You've had them for sixty years. So if you say they are being manipulated, I'm sure you're right. But you have to admit, the staff is doing an excellent job. How carefully they're reinserting the paper into the frame. No smudges on the glass. Rose thought for a moment. You're right, she said, they are doing an excellent job. And she never complained about the staff again. I think this offers us a model of the art critic, if not an itinerary for art criticism, during a crisis in long-term care. Have you noticed how many stories about the power of art are really about the power of institutions, showrooms of the spirit. Here you are, a traveler in the dark. Its most prominent feature is a retractable shell. I prefer the corrosion of metals to the fading of dyes, less the end of an era than its bedtime. Someday it will have to be told how anti-Stalinism, which started out more or less as Trotskyism, turned into art for art's sake, and thereby cleared the way, heroically, for what was to come: Nuisance animals climbing honeycomb structures. Fentanyl overdose vids. I'm studying how glare light scatters in the eye. I'm tracking how expressions of dissatisfaction with the given world can be recuperated by sonic patterning. The bruised idealism of the nectarine. Before a physical confrontation, the girls at my high school used to remove their rings. A ceremony of great solemnity and tenderness. Like one of those children's singing games that's also an artifact of pagan survivalism. Eccentric circles, clapping, buffoonery. Or like a candle visualization relaxation technique designed to counter the gender panic threatening meaningful interdisciplinarity. Sample sentences, pop-up affects. We were walking on the beach at sunset, hoping to see a green flash. My cousin was explaining a difficulty in his marriage, which he kept referring to as a "sticking point." I feel less like I'm living my life, he said, than displaying my life's elements. That he didn't attempt to kill the mosquito that had landed on his arm struck me as an indication of the depth of his depression. It was then that I began to ask: What do the things we spare reveal. Now I ask that at the end of every session. It was then I noticed a gunmetal drone hovering a few feet above us. The atmosphere bends the sunlight, separating the light into its colors, much like a prism bends and splits sunlight into rainbows. That way abstraction can rise again. I told him: I think you're confusing two accidents, those of birth and those of glass. Any long-term relationship is going to involve weeping, crizzling, spalling. If conservators had their way, nothing would ever be exhibited in the atrium. Every minute near sunset, brightness changes by a factor of two, so an error of sixty seconds can do permanent damage. He nodded absently, the fentanyl having its effect. At cloud tops, over distant mountains, beneath very strong thermal inversions at high latitudes: little star. I can feel it getting away from me. A sense of ripe conditions, but not for anything. A sense of oceans and old trees. Then a powerful institution approached a friend of mine about curating an exhibition based on their permanent collection. You can have, they said, free rein. Over the course of a year, she drew up plans for a show organized around the halo. How do depictions of the halo change as pictorial space grows complex. When are halos only light and when do they possess implied mass. Are some figures aware of their halos or are they always extradiegetic. She wouldn't really talk about anything else, even as her partner's condition worsened. But increasingly there were problems with the institution; shipping, for instance, was a sticking point. The radiant discs have to be continuously irrigated. Sterile ice has to be packed into the cavities. You have to come up with a fair scoring system for pediatric candidates. Finally, we were having our monthly lunch, and she was complaining, as ever, about the staff, when I just kind of blurted out: Emma, it's never going to happen. Olivia, it's a pipe dream. Mia, there's just no way. All of the most popular baby names end in *a*. As in sparkling rosé. Wild fennel pollen. Stone fruit tossed with salt, bay leaf, and coriander seeds. Think of the head as the lid of a pot, holding the flavor of the shrimp inside its body. Isla, Olivia, Aurora, Cora, Ada, Amara, I said, as she started to cry. The water in our glasses trembled as the G train passed beneath us, little perturbations in the medium. Someday it will have to be told how spider monkeys, who started out more or less as woolly monkeys, evolved a distinct system of locomotion, and thereby cleared the way, heroically, for what was to come: Anonymity networks. Among my friends, at least my guy friends, a return to traditional prosody. But of course we never talk about me; we talk about whether you're going to get shit on Twitter for folding in the aureola. Is it better to be sponsored by the diocese or Big Tobacco. Can we secure a couple of big names for the catalog. Bring me up to speed about your volunteer work at the hospital, you say, when the espressos arrive. Meanwhile your partner is sinking deeper into her memory foam, texting you the latest article about microdosing. Maybe this will help, sad emoji. The self-absorption is staggering. The orator aims to bend the spirit by his speech. Rhythm shapes feeling. I pushed my chair back, a gesture totally unlike me, and threw a couple of twenties on the table. Then I found myself on Fulton Street, dazed in winter sun, more than a little drunk. Only when I dug my hands into my pockets and touched the unfamiliar gloves did I realize I'd taken someone else's black wool coat. But I couldn't just go back into the restaurant after the scene I'd made. I headed toward Fort Greene Park and sat on one of the benches near DeKalb. I felt around the pockets of the coat and found a pack of Vogue cigarettes, the slim British ones marketed to women. While I smoked, I looked through the wallet, which I'd located in the inside pocket. Cash, cards, dry-cleaning ticket, etc. There was also a piece of brown paper which I unfolded, revealing the following handwritten note in purple ink: I know we've had a difficult year, but I want you to know that I love you. I will always love you. What happened in Denver will never happen again. If anything, it has only clarified how important you are to me. I think the way things started was confusing—your being my teacher. And then when my career took off the dynamic was suddenly reversed. The change was hard for both of us, especially with all the travel. I also see now how it stirred up a lot of stuff from childhood. I just started questioning everything.

I'm sure this happens in any long-term relationship, but maybe it's worse now, for our generation, because of climate change. Anyway, I'm not trying to excuse what I did. I just want you to know that I believe in you and I believe in us and I'm looking forward to the adventures the new year will bring. I looked up from the note with tears in my eyes. A siren receded in the distance. The sun seemed suddenly lower in the sky. A large white dog on a leash brushed against my legs as it passed. All of my anger was gone. The message, I felt, was meant for me; folk music is for all of us.

MERIDIAN RESPONSE

The nearly audible click of snow
             on snow, click
of eye contact, tingling
in the scalp that moves
slowly down the neck, sound
heated until it changes
             state, tense
liquid in the mouth, cadence
             falling on

and on, the breath
             colliding with
the pane, inaudible
click of the tongue against
the alveolar ridge, sunlight falling
around a helpless thing.
             This is a recording
of rain stopping, power being cut, room
             tone you take

outside, release into the trees, silver
             leaves
shifting in the dark, the almost
sound when deer look up, small
roots dangling from their mouths,
scattering earth,
             ashes, light
scattering the sound
             of opening the throat

as if to speak.
          I want to make that sound
of setting something down
on paper as opposed to under
glass, ghostly opposition, vowel
of stone fruit
          softening, whisper of internal
inflammation, want to praise
          the low

grade euphoria produced by making fine
          distinctions, click
of tiny differences, bow
drawn across a metal plate
covered with a fine
layer of sand, a nodal pattern, feeling
          forms around
the static, crinkling
          paper, thin

plastics, nymphs
          hatching in
grasses, feeding on grasses, the paper curls
up in flame, attracting
mates. When a near rhyme is lost to slow
changes in pronunciation, a call goes out
          for work
to reconstruct it:
          love

and *move*, alterations in
        the mouth, play
of colors, friends conduct
experiments in hearing
as: distortion *as*
music, ocean *as* traffic, wind in the trees
        like overheard
speech. The not yet audible sound of me
        clinging to belief

in new senses, making
        the softest
possible claim, brushing it against
the grain, taking on a negative
charge so changes might be rung without
waking anybody up,
        sound of pins and needles,
rustle of
        of.

THE DARK THREW PATCHES DOWN UPON ME ALSO

It was not my intention to travel in time,
watch him distribute dried fruit and sweet
crackers to soldiers in hospital, small sums,
writing their letters, this was back when
you might take it to a cousin to be read
under a cut glass lamp. Why do articles fall out
over time, or get put back in, is that a good
question for the poet if I meet him abroad, aboard
one of several no longer extant ferries?
I am an alien here with a residency, light
alien to me, true hawks starting from the trees
at my footfall on gravel, sunburnt from reading
Specimen Days on the small porch across
the street from where another poet died
or began dying. Some residents request it,
others request not to be assigned it, I
made no requests, but still end up traveling
by tram across wartime Manhattan when
the bridge was probably the tallest structure.
No, it wouldn't be completed until, wouldn't
have been completed yet, those are still
my favorite tenses, moths around streetlights
obscuring the casualty lists I'm trying to read
aloud to citizens in formal dress, address,
attempting to stay cool and extant.
I don't make any sense in the high desert,
grip the yellow can with a toothed wheel,
find, instead of coffee, ash, particulate, but
brew it and walk over with a cup for him.

Wake and reread the section about gifts:
it might be worse to love both sides in a war,
a general engagement in the woods, to speak
of a wound's "neighborhood" as they remove
splinters of bone, worse to admire singing
through candlelit gauze than to ignore
a wedding party struck by unmanned drones:
I know no one involved except everyone,
let alone love. They are dead in different ways,
these poets, but I visit them both because
a residency affords me time, not sure where
the money comes from, or what money is,
how you could set it beside a soldier's bed
then walk out across the moonlit mall in love
with the federal, wake up refreshed and bring
tobacco to those who haven't received
wounds in the lung or the face. Tonight
I listen to their recordings at once
in separate windows, four lines from "America"
might be recited by an actor, but the noise
of the wax cylinder is real, sounds how I
imagine engines of old boats would, while
"The Door" incorporates distress into the voice,
could be in the room. The former says
he waits for me ahead, but I doubt I'll arrive
in time: even the phrase "evening papers"
will need a gloss, like the notion presidents
have features. Instead I project myself back
before carbon arc and mercury vapor, invisible

labor of men in the dimly lit caissons
still a few years in the future, when the danger
will be coming up too fast, nitrogen
bubbles forming in the blood. I wanted to say
I also pass through a series of air locks en route
to imperceptible work, even that a tower of a sort
might be built upon it, but I'm more a supervisor
ill from surfacing quickly, watching its progress
through a telescope, sending messages to
the bridge site through my good wife, Emily.
When completed, the celebration will surpass
the one that marked the closing of the war, as if
you could separate those things, as if those were
things, cheap oak and iron deployed
as inflation rages. My father studied briefly
with Hegel, and there are other proper names
we could summon: both Cranes, the one
who lived in this apartment, drowned
himself at my age, and the older one who died
younger, having both seen and not seen war.
But that's just the game of features again,
when in fact the unwounded face is smooth.

A thin crescent hangs over a Brooklyn where
the rich still farm and I wait for your return
from a war you love all sides of: Come back
to the future where I'm resident and the phrase
evokes one of the crucial movies of my youth
set in 1955, the year nuclear power first

lit up a town, Arco, Idaho, also home to the first
meltdown (1961), although years are part
of the game. In the movie they lack plutonium
to power the time-traveling car, whereas
in real life it seeps into the Fukushima soil,
Back to the Future was ahead of its time,
1985, when I was six and the Royals took
the series, in part because a ridiculous call
forced game seven, Orta clearly out at first
in replays. I can feel it getting away from me
so I leave the house, use the back door to avoid
the other residents, and watch the sun
set through smoke from Arizona fires, "zero
percent contained," wave to a woman bent
over a row of yellow flowers, but she can't
see me: I've faded from the photograph.
We often say "twilight" but mean "dusk,"
or check our watches without noting the time,
two of the minor practices that make us
enough of a people to believe that a raid
on the compound can bring closure. Depends
what you think is ending, the gentle face
of terror, civilian nuclear power, are those
two things? There are men at work on the roof
when I return, too hot to do by day, wave
and am seen, an awkward exchange
in Spanish, who knows what I said, having
confused the conditional with imperfect.
Norteño from their radio fills the house

I hope they know isn't mine: I just write here.
Walk back out with a Brita and three glasses,
but of course they have their own water, can
I offer you a cup of ashes, can I interest you?
Soon they move on to the house I call his
because Douglas, who manages the compound,
rushed him from there to hospital in Midland
or Odessa, the roofers' purpose obscure to me,
whose work is to chat with the dying or dead,
to let them lay a pale hand on my knee
if they still have hands, the practical nurses
busy behind curtains, some of them singing
popular hymns, often accompanied on melodeon,
an accordion or small organ, strange
to have either available among the cots
and mosquito netting. It seems to be pleasurable
for him when the moon makes radiant patches
for a death-stricken boy to moan in, or
a patch of the wood ignites, consuming
soldiers too crippled to flee. "Patch" from
the Latin, *pedaeum*, literally something
measured, compare to the medieval *pedāre*:
to measure in feet. That might be false,
the point is he feels no need to contain his love
for the material richness of their dying, federal
body from which extremities secede, a pail
beside the bed for that purpose, almost never
mentions race, save to note there are plenty
of Black soldiers, clean Black women would

make wonderful nurses, while again and again
I deliver money to boys with perforated organs:
"unionism," to die with shining hair
beside fractional currency, part of writing
the greatest poem. Or is the utopian moment
loving the smell of shit and blood, brandy
as it trickles through the wound, politics of pure
sensation? When you die in the patent office
there's a pun on expiration, you must enter one
of the immense glass cases filled with scale
models of machines, utensils, curios. Look,
your president will be shot in a theater,
actors will be presidents, the small sums
will grow monstrous as they circulate, measure:
I have come from the future to warn you.

Tomorrow I'll see the Donald Judd
permanent installations in old hangars, but
now it's tomorrow and I didn't go, set out hatless
in the early afternoon, got lost and was soon
seeing floaters and spots, so returned to the house,
the interior sea green until my eyes adjusted,
I lay down for a while and dreamt I saw it.
Tonight I'll shave, have two drinks with a friend
of a friend, but that was last week and I canceled,
claimed altitude had sickened me a little, can
we get back in touch when I've adjusted?
Yesterday I saw the Donald Judd in a book
they keep in the house, decided not to go until

I finished a poem I've since abandoned
but will eventually pick back up. What I need
is a residency within the residency, then
I could return refreshed to this one, take in Judd
with friends of friends, watch the little spots
of blood bloom on the neck, so I'll know
I've shaved in time, whereas now I'm as close
to a beard as I've been, but not very close.
Shaving is a way to start the workday by ritually
not cutting your throat when you've the chance,
"Washes and razors for foofoos—
for me freckles and a bristling beard,"
a big part of reading him is embarrassment.
Woke up today having been shaved in a dream
by a nurse who looked like Falconetti,
my cot among the giant aluminum boxes
I still plan to see, then actually shaved and felt
that was work enough for one day, my back
to the future. The foundation is closed
Sundays and nights, of which the residency
is exclusively composed, so plan your visit
well in advance, or just circle the building
where the Chamberlain sculptures are housed,
painted and chromium-plated steel, best
viewed through your reflection in the window:
In Bastien-Lepage's *Joan of Arc* (1879)
she reaches her left arm out, maybe for support
in the swoon of being called, but instead
of grasping branches or leaves, her hand,

in what is for me the crucial passage, partially
dissolves. It's carefully positioned
on the diagonal sightline of one of three
hovering, translucent angels he was attacked
for failing to reconcile with the future saint's
realism, a "failure" the hand presents
as a breakdown of space, background
beginning to swallow her fingers, reminding me
of the photograph people fade from, the one
"Marty" uses to measure the time remaining
for the future in which we watched the movie,
only here it's the future's presence, not
absence that eats away at her hand: you can't
rise from the loom so quickly that you
overturn the stool and rush toward the plane
of the picture without startling the painter, hear
voices the medium is powerless to depict
without that registering somewhere on the body.
But from our perspective, it's precisely
where the hand ceases to signify a hand
and is paint, no longer appears to be warm
or capable, that it reaches the material
present, becomes realer than sculpture because
tentative: she is surfacing too quickly.
This is why her face is in my dream, not hers,
but the beautiful actress that played her (1928),
also because in the film she recants her false
confession, achieves transcendence
only after her head is shaved. I'm embarrassed

because there are workers on the roof
for whom this is the north, and no one calls
from beyond the desert frame except a poet
or two, the conflict between two systems
of incompatible labor endures, and the third
is the flickering border between them,
the almost-work of taking everything personally
until the person becomes a commons,
a radical "loafing" that embraces the war
because it also dissolves persons, a book
that aspires to the condition of currency. Warhol
wanted to make a movie of *Specimen Days*.

Some say the glowing spheres near Route 67
are paranormal, others dismiss them as
atmospheric tricks: static, swamp gas, reflections
of headlights and small fires, but why dismiss
what misapprehension can establish, our own
illumination returned to us as alien, as sign?
They've built a concrete viewing platform
lit by low red lights that must appear
mysterious when seen from what it overlooks.
Tonight I see no spheres, but project myself
and then gaze back, an important trick because
the goal is to be on both sides of the poem,
shuttling between the you and I. But what
is the mystery he claims his work both does
and doesn't contain, what does he promise,
say we have silently accepted, cannot state,

and how is it already accomplished as we read,
and who is being addressed in the last stanza
of "Crossing Brooklyn Ferry"? Form
is always the answer to the riddle it poses, though
there isn't much of one here, just a speaker
emptied of history so he can ferry across it:
tide, wake, barge, flag, foundry are things
anyone could see, but no one in particular,
less things than examples of things, which once
meant a public meeting place, assembly.
Words are the promise he can't make
in words without rendering them determinate
and thereby breaking the promise because
only when empty can we imagine assembling,
not as ourselves, but as representatives
of the selves he has asked us to dissolve:
dumb ministers. These are the contradictory
conditions of my residency in the poem,
where Ari isn't allowed to join me because
she's from the world, and what I miss most
is the distortion, noise of the wax cylinder,
the flaws in the medium that preserve
what distance it closes, source of the glow
I return to Creeley for. I wanted to include
her daily reports on how the lavender held up
throughout the heat wave, the dilated root
where my aorta meets my heart, how I mistook
two moths drawn to the flashlight for
the eyeshine of some animal approaching

in the dark, good to know that I can still
feel an almost sexual terror on these meds.
Then I had big plans for stinging ants
as a figure of collectivity experienced
as weird fact of the privileged residency,
wasted a morning baiting them with apple,
blushing hard when Douglas asked. Don't ask:
the visiting painter's diastema, the vaguely
erotic pity in her smile, the altitude-induced
nosebleed that I slept through, beard of blood
in the bathroom mirror, terrible phrase
stuck in my head for a week, the chances of
distant recurrence somewhere in my mother,
small rain on the skylight, having learned
to distinguish begging calls of baby swallows
from the chatter of adults. A friend in California
believes he is breathing in hot particles
from Fukushima, where a rabbit has been born
without ears, should I include that here
along with the other casualties, or will
everything be leveled as soon as it appears
in the catalog? My favorite part of the book:
he's in Topeka and is supposed to read
a poem to twenty thousand people, instead
decides to write a speech he fails to give
because he's having a great time at dinner,
so he just puts the speech in the book where we
can read it at our leisure, makes you wonder
if he actually sent the letter he included

written to a dead soldier's mother. Whitman:
poetry replaced by oratory addressed
to the future, the sensorial commons
abandoned for a private meal. If only there were
more wandering away from the stage, less
tallying, one of his favorite verbs, I could
turn to him now, but the reflection
of his head is haloed by spokes of light, "cross"
is in the title, and there are other signs
of a negative incarnation, paper heaven
where the suffering is done by others.
I've been worse than unfair, although he was
asking for it, is still asking for it, I can hear
him asking for it through me when I speak,
despite myself, to a people that isn't there,
or think of art as leisure that is work
in houses the undocumented build, repair.
It's among the greatest poems and fails
because it wants to become real and can
only become prose, founding mistake
of the book from which we've been expelled.
And yet: look out from the platform, see
mysterious red lights move across the bridge
in a Brooklyn I may or may not return to,
phenomena no science can explain,
wheeled vehicles rushing through the dark
with their windows down, streaming music.

THE CAMPERDOWN ELM

Our children do not mean
Their numbers are up, the fireflies
To kill them when they cup
Around the soft bodies, light
Music softens features
The way a mild solvent
Softens the acrylic, yellowing in time

The old habit of sentience
After a storm, the light
I've come to feel ok ascribing
Features, the Camperdown Elm
Because it was celebrated in a poem
They've put a gate around
Cupped it, as a friend

Is cupped, heated glass along
The meridians of her body, slow
Release of energy, she is in
Sustainable agony most of the time
I place a firefly in each cup
I place them in the branches of
And ask it to watch over her

The grafted elm, its weeping habit
Even though the light is cold
The wings damaged, cupped
Flame of it, the toddler says
The surface varnish has dissolved

She wants to know if it makes honey
That glows in the dark, slow

Pulse of it, the intervals
Shorter on warm nights, it won't
Kill you, the pathetic fallacy
My August fallacy, so that fall
So that September has a flaw
In the glass of it, where it catches, is
Damaged lightly and released

Walking at dusk through the long meadow, recording this on my phone, that's my job, as old as soldiery, the hills, the soldered hills where current flows, green current. When you are finished recording, your lips are dried flowers. The trees are full of black plastic bags and hornets' nests, but not significance; the task of imbuing them falls to me. And it's me, Ben, just calling to check in. I'm on the way to pick Marcela up from daycare and wanted to hear about your trip. I'm sure it must have been hard seeing him like that. Anyway, I love you and I'm here. Give me a call when you can. I'll be around until the late nineteenth century, when carved wood gives way to polished steel, especially in lake surfaces. You know how you sometimes realize it has been raining only when it stops, silence falling on the roof, forming rivulets on the glass? This is the religious equivalent of that, especially in music and applied fields, long meadows. Overwintering queens make wonderful pets, just don't expect them to understand your writing, how you've rearranged the stresses to sponsor feelings in advance of the collective subject who might feel them, good work if you can get it, and you can't, nobody can, that's why the discipline is in crisis, this cut-flower business, applied folds, false equivalence. I remember when I interviewed for this position. I was wearing a Regency trimmed velvet tailcoat with a small hole over the left breast where the lead ball had entered one of my great-grandfather's five heart-like structures. I met the committee at a Hyatt. The room had migraine carpet; a conventional river scene hung above the bed. After the usual pleasantries, the chairperson requested that I sing and soon the painted water began to flow. It's hard to believe that was over two hundred years ago, when people still got dressed up for air travel and children were expected to absorb light in their super-black feathers, making contour disappear. They probably evolved to startle predators, make us seem deep, so that, when they least expected it, we could cast their underground nests with molten aluminum, sell them online as sculpture. But if you've ever seen a dendritic pattern in a frozen pond, lightning captured in hard plastic, or the delicate venation of an insect wing (the fourth vein of the wing is called the media), then you've probably felt that a spirit is at work in the world, or was, and that making it visible is the artist's task, or was. I am resolved to admire all elaborate silvery pathways no matter where I find them, that's why I'm calling. I'm sitting in Grand Army Plaza by the fountain, which they've shut off until the spring, when it will again give sensuous expression to our freedom. In other words, I'm at work, realigning and interlocking barbules, lubricating what are essentially dead structures with a fatty oil I've developed for that purpose, thinking of you, holding you in my thoughts like fireflies in glass, cold to the touch, green current. You just can't blame yourself. The last time I saw him we had dinner in Fort Greene and he was cracking me up with his impressions, especially of John. He was drinking, but not too much: one cocktail, white wine. The only weird moment was when I had to look at my phone because I was getting a lot of texts and wanted to make sure everything was ok with the girls. He kind of freaked out about it: Am I boring you, do you need to make a call. But I apologized and we moved on. What reassured me most was how excited he was about the new job, even if it didn't pay much. They were going to let him use the 3D printers for some of his own stuff and he was really psyched about that. Anyway, I love you and I'm here. I've got to get Marcela now but tonight I'm around, promoting syllables, trying to avoid the twin traps of mere procedure and sentimentalism, ingesting around seventeen milligrams, blunt toothed leaves in motion lights, signifying nothing, but holding a place. Lately my daughters have been asking what I do when they're at school; I want to say I enchant the ferryman with my playing so that lost pets may return, that the magnet tiles arrange themselves into complex hexagonal structures at my song, but they know I'm not the musical one, that I describe the music of others, capture it in hard plastic. With the profits I purchase an entrapping foam that coats the nest for a complete kill and a pendant that resembles a tiny abacus of pearls, responsibly sourced. What does a normal day look like for you? For me the fruit is undefined around the edges and the faces of some friends are mere suggestions while others observe the standard codes of verisimilitude in a way that feels increasingly affected; why appear vividly when it's dusk, has been dusk for ages. I don't know if oysters can feel pain, can't even know if other humans do, although I recognize what philosophers call "pain behavior" among my loved ones as the seasons change. Tie their stems together with unflavored dental floss and hang them upside down, but display them away from windows or they'll fade, polished steel gives way to painted water, a turn of phase, a change of phrase, the slippages release small energy and the harvest falls to me. Someday I'd like to bring my daughters to work, but not today. Today is cut glass flowers reinforced internally with wire, a vibration control system, the religious equivalent of that, lampwork they're too young to understand, the effects too mild. Their nests are paper, they can discriminate between fragments of foreign and natal comb, the interests between workers and their queen diverge, those are the three prerequisites for song, for the formation of singers who will eat both meat and nectar, which they feed to larvae on the bus ride home. Marcela pulls the yellow stop-request cord, but never hard enough, so you have to help without her knowing, say great job. Say great job to the sensible world if you want to encourage reenchantment, keep the trees in touch with their strengths, the magnolia's increasing northern range, for instance, soon to be cold-hardy beyond zone four. The way we say of our children "they went down" to mean they fell asleep, that makes me glass, soft glass bending in long meadows, a fallacy each generation reinvents and disavows, reinvents and disavows, a rocking motion. Otherwise you're mixing pills and gin and your friends are debating if it constitutes a true attempt, recklessness, a cry for help, before deciding it makes no difference, it's pain behavior, he has to be checked in, monitored, sponsored, set to music. Anyway, the girls are down and I can talk. I'm just clicking on things in bed, a review by a man who says I have no feelings and hate art. Through the blinds I can see the blue tip of the neighbor's vape pen signaling in the dark, cold firefly. The raccoons are descending from their nests in foreclosed attics to roam the streets of Kensington, we moved last summer, have a guest room now, come visit. I can't believe I haven't seen you since his wedding.

THE READERS

Love brought these readers into the world
The cuplike structures
of their eyes were formed
inherited color, and love
and argument must be conducted differently now
that the sounds through the wall
are interpreted, and a gentle

relentless pressure has been placed
on the page. I paid someone to care for them so I
could pattern these vowels and one
is eight and asking me each
night to read what I've made
in what they call my office
I am afraid

they will understand it or won't, will see
something they should
not remember when I'm gone, the voice that is
mine only in part must be kept
safe from them. They are too trivial
my offices, too intimate, it isn't labor
I cannot bring my daughters to work

or not bring them
here. They have learned to pause
at the end of lines, they want to know if I have met
Amanda Gorman, debate
if it has to rhyme and what rhyme is

is difference, segmentation, how emphasis falls
is brushed away. So I keep

two notebooks, one where I write
for them in the half
hour before pickup, while this one holds a place
or no place where it breaks, I'm not sure what
open. Desire they cannot know
and will, the sense of false position
for which I've been rewarded, this house, fantasy

I had at her age that my father was
replaced by a man who resembled him
is a cliché, the words
the faces interchangeable
of the father. But soon they began to blur
together in my mind
because the rhyme my girls

demanded spread, as difference tends
and sameness. So I read from the wrong one
what I'd been working on
and it was this, the changes I've made
were these, and the love I gave
received. Though it wasn't a game or song
they played and sang along

Then she suggested I make a list of all the things I'm grateful for. No entry is too small or mundane: access to clean water, fast internet, the weeping habit of the flowering cherry. And you can be grateful for what you don't have, she explained, lice or colorblindness. A friend in Bellevue. A daughter in pain. We were sitting on a bench in Green-Wood Cemetery, sitting as far away from each other as possible. It was late April and I could just pick out the song of nearby warblers from the distant, constant sirens. But it's important you make the list by hand, there's something crucial about the physical contact with the paper, the embodied act of mark making, she explained. And each sentence must start the same way—"I'm grateful for"—the repetition helps form a groove in your consciousness so that, when idle, your mind will gravitate toward an awareness of its blessings instead of the darker ruminations you're describing. Males sing a slow, soft trill. It lasts about three seconds. I suggest making the list at the same time each day, I make mine in the morning, but I have clients who make them at night, right before bed, just ten or fifteen minutes of writing, set a timer on your phone. Whereas the ovenbird, named for its domed nest, sings: *teacher, teacher, teacher.* I was trying to locate the rage in my body, to greet the rage so it would dissipate, trying not to ask out loud: Is that what I am to you, another client? Instead I asked: Is the list aspirational, can I list things I *want* to feel grateful for, *should* feel grateful for, or does the gratitude, at the time of writing, need to be an accomplished fact, available to feeling? She looked at me to ascertain if I was being serious or merely difficult, but I did not turn my head to meet her gaze, didn't want to see the patient smile, the diastema. A gust of wind provoked a rain of pale, white blossoms onto the stone path, but the tree's stock of blossoms did not appear diminished. The rage, which I'd experienced as lodged in my temples and the back of my neck, turned now to unalloyed sorrow, which lives in my chest. Aspirational is fine, she said. Aspirational is great. The word "aspirational" brought out her Argentinian accent. She coughed twice, and I imagined airborne droplets traveling from her mouth to mine, or entering my body through my eyes, pathways to the soul, and I welcomed that, was grateful for it, wondered if I would get an erection and, if so, would I be able to hide it from her if she stood suddenly and wanted to continue birding. My brother is colorblind, I said. Nobody had any idea until we drove to St. Louis one weekend and visited this place called the Magic House, a kind of science center for kids. I was seven and he was ten. There was a room there, almost a gallery, where they displayed a variety of those "digit tests"—circles formed by dots of different sizes. Inside the pattern dots of a distinct color form a number invisible to those with a particular color deficiency. My brother kept saying he couldn't see anything in the circles and while at first my parents thought he was joking, I could tell that something suddenly clicked for them. How many times had they asked him for the red marker and been handed the green one. How many times had the otherwise perspicacious kid failed to circle the yellow bird in the math worksheet. Maybe this is why for as long as I've been looking at paintings I always feel like a deficiency might be revealed, aesthetic experience is tinged with that anxiety for me, the way the blossoms are tinged with pink. But I also remember being really jealous of my brother, his specialness, his difference, maybe because my parents, guilty for having failed to diagnose their son, subtly favored him for a few months, or maybe because of what happened in one of the next rooms at the Magic House. There was a wall that consisted almost entirely of safes with combination locks. This room was crowded with people trying random combinations, trying to open one of the safes. On the wall was a list of the probabilities of arriving at the right permutation for the respective locks. The point was it was nearly impossible. And yet this was one of the most popular rooms in the Magic House. Certainly my brother and I were instantly mesmerized, trying random numbers again and again, refusing to give any other kid a chance at our safe, even though the wall text said the safes were empty. I don't know how long we spent in the safe room, which had the frenetic feel of a video game arcade, or people playing the slots, that kind of mania, but at a certain point I heard, I remember hearing, my brother's safe make a satisfying click. Everyone gasped, fell silent, and watched as the small, heavy door swung open. You're making this up, she said. And out of the darkness of the safe burst forth seven parrot finches with bright green bodies and red heads, birds I thought my brother couldn't see, believing as I did that being colorblind meant you couldn't perceive the colored object, not just an aspect of its surface. If my brother were here today, he would see stone paths making their way through empty space, none of this vibrating green, and he would hear all the notes of birdsong at once. I turned toward her suddenly, involuntarily, and said, my anger unmistakable: I'm grateful for colorblindness, the missing cones, the hidden figure. I'm grateful you and your family are moving to Buenos Aires for a while; I'm sure you'll never want for clients. She looked at me with a vaguely erotic pity, took a sip of chamomile tea from her paper cup, a cup she'd brought from home, not a café, cafés hadn't reopened yet, but which seemed store-bought, as if she had access to an open city. A couple of years ago, she began, Luna had lice. She'd been itching for a while, but it wasn't until the school sent out an email reporting lice in the kindergarten classroom that it occurred to me to check. When I went through her masses of curly black hair with a steel comb and a flashlight, I was shocked: I found not only lots of nits, dots of different sizes, but plenty of live insects moving around her hair. I felt guilt, a mother is a machine for making guilt. I tried to comb them out and bought that medicated shampoo. She slept with a plastic shower cap, which was very cute. A couple of days later we got another email about the ongoing lice situation from the "class parent," who said that many of the moms also now had lice, that's what we get from all that cuddling (smiley face emojis, exclamation points). But I didn't have any lice, even though Luna's scalp was an open city, and now I wondered if this meant we weren't cuddling sufficiently, that I wasn't being affectionate enough physically, which sounds crazy when I say it, given how often we're entangled, but at the time we were trying to set some firm limits about her coming into our bed at night. I was a bad mother for failing to notice her itching, the lice, a worse mother for having failed to contract lice myself, for having banned her from our bed. This was all overdetermined for me because lice—for my grandparents and so for my parents—meant the camps. Had I abandoned my family in Argentina; certainly I'd abandoned Judaism; I was a failed daughter failing my daughter. Don't make a joke about psychoanalysis, Ben—I'd opened my mouth to speak—I'm not making an argument, I'm describing a feeling. The shampoo didn't work, there were more nits than I could remove, so I googled what to do: it turns out the expert lice pickers in New York are all Orthodox Jews, mainly in Midwood, it's fascinating, I can send you the *Times* article about it, and so I just chose this woman who had the best Yelp reviews. That night I got into bed with Luna, didn't even wait for her to come to my room, and we slept cheek to cheek. You're making this up, I said. I wanted the lice to connect me to my predecessors and my progeny. The next day, when this young woman—long black dress, her hair covered with a scarf—picked a louse from my hair, held it to the light, I was so happy, tears started in my eyes. The woman thought I was ashamed of myself and tried to comfort me. You have so many things to be grateful for, she said. Your beautiful daughter, your home, running water, that lice can be killed on the Sabbath, even though it's a day of rest, an exception issuing from the ancient rabbis' belief that lice are spontaneously created from dust. She took a sip of her tea, which must have been cold. Something stirred in the towering oak behind us, maybe a raccoon raiding a nest for eggs. I looked up and saw a plane moving slowly across the sky, a ghost flight, an empty or nearly empty plane following an established route so the carrier can retain its slots at airports. The white streaks on the warbler's back are tinged with olive, the darker ruminations tinged with gold. Repetition forms a groove.

DILATION

1

We need to harness the vaguely erotic disappointment that attends
    the realization you aren't being followed,
keys gripped between the fingers, ready to strike at the eyes
The afterimage of Byzantine gold leaf dissolving in the trees when
    we emerge from the museum must be harnessed,
and the delicate carnation of the sky at the rooftop screening,
and the dress of the hostess, its exploration of formative drives

If you are anything like me, you emerge from the hospital's
    automatic doors into the heat and glare of its parking lot
unable to recall the color of the rental or the demands of practical
    reason
You surface from the subway to find it's fully night and hard to
    remember the preceding generation's claims
for disjunction, you saw the child of a Turkish diplomat fall from a
    penthouse balcony,
curled up on a floor model at the SoHo Crate & Barrel when you
    received the terrible news

from a poem that probably dates from 1939, address to an adjacent
    posterity
Green eyeshadow and surprising gentleness of the saleswoman who
    asks if I'm ok must be harnessed if we
are to surpass camp and apathy, plainclothes security closing in
You feel emancipated briefly from fragmentation when the D train
    emerges onto the Manhattan Bridge,
vertically polarized light entering the water, seventy-six stories of
    rippled steel refusing to be actual

all at once, stand and offer your seat to an old man who isn't there,
    listen politely to his demand for a theater
that combines distance and empathy, false proscenium lit to reveal
evaporating value, the delicate carnation that follows heat and glare

2

I came into the cities at a time when stray military transmissions
   were confused for signs of alien life, a kind of poetry
I came into the cities at a time in which all but the poorest among us
   had been colonized by blue light
In the midst of weather patterns of increasing extremity, I came into
   the cities, water trembling in my glass
as the G passed underneath me, notes of chlorine, antidepressants in
   trace amounts
One way was enumerating the bad forms of alienated collective
   power: breathing hot particles from Japan,

bundled debt, another way was passing beyond the reach of friends,
   to internalize an allegory,
tracking the dilation where aorta meets heart, minor tremor in the
   hand
Part of me wants to say there is a mock-oratorical mode capable of
   vitalizing critical agency and part of me
wants to praise the maple's winged samaras, the distance achieved
   from the parent tree,
but mainly I want to argue they're one thing, real if indefensible

like cities in time, spinning as they fall
My role in the slaughter doesn't disqualify the beauty I find in all
   forms of sheltered flame, little votive polis,
that I eat while others starve does not refute the promise of
   dimming houselights, weird fullness of the instant
before music, that I ventriloquize when I address you *is* the marker
   of my voice, important source
of syrup and tonewood, coming to you live

from the ellipses of compotier and vase, grave air of a masterpiece,
    its notes of ozone and exhaust,
jasmine in trace amounts, tracking the dilation of new forms
of private temporality into public architecture, glass curtains as they
    dim

3

The ideal is visible through its antithesis like small regions of warm
    blue underpainting and this is its late
July realization, I'm sorry, I know you were expecting more
I'm not going to lecture the neighbor kid with the hydrant key
    about conserving water for posterity
until I can think of a better idea for the spontaneous formation of a
    public, however brief
By the time you read this, if you are close enough to read this, if you
    are reading this

a threat to the first person was called in, prompting its evacuation, a
    panic you should take advantage of
in order to compose a face, test predicates against, walk to Sunset
    Park and watch the soft-winged kites
at magic hour when light appears immanent to the lit, warm blue
    scattering
in the gaps between buildings and print, you can feel the content
    streaming
The ideal is a kind of longitudinal subject in which the poem is a
    note saying where I left you keys

and a bottle of green wine, sea-rise visible in the compound eye,
    mosaic image, flicker effect
in which objects must move in order to persist, thus the preference
    of bees for windblown flowers,
thus the analogy collapses like a colony, prompting its evacuation,
    but the formal capacity for likening still shines
through its antithesis, feel it misfiring, vaguely erotic disappointment
    that combines

distance and empathy, carnation fading from the contrails, trying to
    conceive

in a ready-to-assemble bed as the metropole shifts East
I believe there is a form of apology both corporate and incantatory
    that could convene the future it begs for leniency,
inherited dream you can put anything in: antithetical blue, predicate
    green

THE PISTIL

Now that nothing has been done
Before, you can speak of the stigma
       style and ovary
Fourth whorl of the flower
You can run your tongue
Along the lips of the sleeping
No one has touched
Your hair, described the fall of it
Now you can smoke
Indoors, around your daughters
Windows open to spring
Nights that flare up in winter
Words like transparent
Shells attached to the elms
       maples and ash
I hear the people
Because tonight is recycling
Picking through glass
As I write you, slow pour of metal
Into the mold, my speech direct
Because recycled
The prohibition against
Feeling broken like bread
Above the sill, an inferior mirage
Above their heads, minute gaps
Impulses pass through, blue
       sparks rise in the dark
Fourth wall of the flower
Splits at maturity, releases

Sentiment, follicle fruit of it, soft
Space between bones of the skull
Where dreams are knitting
Delicate fallacies, now that bees
The coral and ice, white
Noses of bats, it's time
To write the first poem in English
Each line the last, small
           rain turning glass

Sometimes you have to kill the bee, my father would say. Sometimes you have to press the flower. The proverbs he quoted made at least as much sense to me as the ones my grandmother claimed were Yiddish: Fleas are not lobsters. He can make the dream larger than the night. After my father died, I found that I was using some of these phrases in my own life. I didn't really think about what they meant. Nobody ever asked me to explain them. One afternoon I was hanging out with Emma—she was so careful I didn't worry about distancing—and I said this thing about the bee and flower and she was like, What are you quoting? What does that mean? They're just sayings. Idiomatic expressions. Clichés. I don't think so, she said. Where did you learn them? And I told her. And that's when I realized: the blue path never curves. That's when I realized, or realized in a new way, that stars are not steeples. The nouns are interchangeable. The dream that presses the flower spares the bee. Soon we were drinking red wine and googling these sayings I'd believed connected me to my father and through my father to Ukraine and Judaism, personal and collective histories; in fact none of them was timeworn, none had circulated, they were just his private nonsense formulations. I felt like laughing and crying simultaneously. My father was a poet: He made a world for me, a toy folk tradition. Or my father was a fraud: How else had he deceived me? Or my father was a comedian: He knew I'd figure it out in the end and find it funny. And I did find it funny, I was laughing in Emma's arms while also shaking with sobs, blowing my nose on her shirt, maybe just missing my ridiculous dad. Outside her window we could hear the protesters gathering on DeKalb, but that night we wouldn't join them. Emma started making up her own expressions as she held me, stroked my hair. Seven days from now is not a future. Don't buy a mattress during vespers. One iris is always a different color than the other. At first, her delivery was mock-portentous, but then she got into it, there was something hypnotic about it, soothing. When I was half-asleep I half believed that I could hear the protesters chanting the phrases that Emma was coining just for me: We are the glass that plates the wound. The rain enters the dream as snow. The rose is absolute. A call and response between the whisper in my ear and the people in the streets. Even though it was muffled by a mask, I could pick out my father's voice.

THE CIRCUIT

1

Suppose that we hit the body
with a tremendous, whether it's ultraviolet
or just very powerful light, supposing you brought the light
inside the body, which you can do either
through the skin or in some other way
Suppose the source of the light is moving
past the body, forming a dark fringe
around the empty center, still place
Below the range of human hearing
Whether they were the mating calls of insects
sonic weapons, a pressure was experienced
at the short wavelength, with a tremendous
Let us suppose, then, that we are dreaming
violet you can drink

through the skin. I was at the embassy
without my knowledge, I came forward with my symptoms
Light sensitivity, malaise, checking my phone
A dry coughing sound high up in the trees
and was dismissed until they saw the scans
the shadows, it was as though I had sustained
a secret life in my sleep, the damage was clear
water running over stones, stock imagery where
memory should be. I heard
hail on the roof of the train at Ninth
and Carroll, but when I emerged at Fifteenth, the sky
there was no evidence, but pellets of white ice
along the curb, in the streetlight, the grass
at the edge of the park, I saw her and

she held a handful toward me, Here
I have been saving this for you since the pandemic began
and I took it, I experienced it as warm
ice she pressed into my hand, warm ice is a thing
I made a note to remember, the press of her
is a thing now, and we sat on the bench
Listening to the rats in the ground cover
music from passing cars, and she asked me
Is there a way we can do something like that by injection
inside, or almost a cleaning, because you see
it gets in the lungs and it does a tremendous
concept of the light, the way it kills
it in one minute, that's pretty
powerful. People should look into it

2

I am trying to remember what it felt like to believe
disjunction, non sequitur, injection
between sentences might constitute
meaningful struggle against the empire
typing away in my dorm, my roommate
freshman year would get stoned and listen
to classical music on his headphones
he had green hair, and one night he came in very late
I was asleep, and then like I'd been hit
these incredible waves of sound, and I shot up
his eyes were closed, he was conducting
but hadn't plugged them in, and I was screaming
waving my arms, but his eyes
and then I kind of relaxed into it

I am trying to pinpoint the moment where I realized
what seems obvious now, that it doesn't
run on prose, the advertisements
speeches at rallies, the lightning-fast trades
of bundled debt, among the most beautiful phrases
in American English, that you campaign
in conventional verse, but govern in avant-garde
pieties regarding pulling it apart, that what
I grew up thinking was a kind of
Trojan horse in the sense of malware
poets uploaded into language, a small
jamming mechanism for the smooth flow of
information over stones, was in fact
I read a transcript of a Sarah Palin speech

at Penn in 2008 instead of from my book
I was asleep, and then like I'd been hit
a white fantasy, classical. The point is not that the work
wasn't good, or that the writer doesn't have
debts and tactics, but that I am still coming
I love this phrase, to terms
with the fact that the fascist reaction and I
was mimetic of what I thought I opposed
with my typing. The search for new commitments
for a new language of commitment
to inhabit but also refuse, insist
on a domain of contingency, chance, to be disorganized
by desire, no pieties in the arts
and beyond. There are people looking into it

3

Warm ice is a thing
being an ambassador without your knowledge
is a thing, the violet hour of empire is too grand, but there is
when residual sunlight takes on a predominantly blue
shade and there are no sharp
shadows on the scan
an hour (which doesn't last an hour) in which the brightness
of the sky matches streetlights, lit windows
and more light is scattered in the body
and the body is redder and softer for
a brief window is among
the most beautiful phrases changing
phase, valence
I still believe in that

capacity to take it in, not to be cleansed
but to be equal to it for a while
as the kids say, to hold it
and I am still the kids at forty
two, I am still relaxing into looking into it
rushes past and through me, to let it go and hold it
in the moment of composition, to be tense
and relaxed, ready to move, be moved by it
whatever it is, an openness
along the curb, in the streetlight
which is social, a small circuit
a small amount of current flowing

from emitter to base
at dusk between the sentences

and the people
it gets in the lungs

THE THEORY

I've seen the branching drainage pattern produced by snow melt in photographs from space and I have seen the same pattern at my feet. After my uncle's funeral, wearing his scarf, I looked down at the Charles and saw that pattern in the ice. A teardrop-shaped motif on dark blue silk detached from the scarf and is available to me now, when I shut my eyes. (My aunt said the scarf was becoming on me, leaving carbonized patterns, or "tracks," on my neck.) From the initial hexagonal prism, I've seen a wide variety of symmetric shapes growing as they fall, have caught them on my tongue, the spike proteins of the snow binding with memory, producing some immunity, which then fades. I saw an exhibition once of things too sensitive to light to be exhibited and cried my way through it, in fact I see it every morning, the branching crystalized salt in the magnified tear. I knew a woman who had that pattern tattooed on her back, which is where it often occurs naturally if you're struck by lightning (the pattern fades), and I know a woman (Emma) who is stuck in this terrible triangle with her mom and brother, fighting constantly with the former over the latter, the lattice, his crystal habit, and it fell to me to pick him up at JFK. He deplaned in a haze, Xanax probably, and initially we drove in silence—windows cracked despite the cold—back to Fort Greene, where there was an empty apartment he could stay in for a while; he just had to cat sit. I put the radio on and they were talking about the Capitol and soon this stream of language was coming out of him and flowing over the hard and soft rocks between us. (It might be useful here to picture in your mind a brick wall with some cracks that appear in the bricks. The speech erodes the softer rock and flows around the harder rock.) It was all about the deep state and clearance and breadcrumbs, tiny droplets escaping from the edges of the surgical mask. I focused on the rhythmic patterning of his speech to the exclusion of its meaning, which is why, when I was getting off on Tillary Street, it took me a while to realize he was now asking about my uncle, expressing his condolences, expressing—for the first time in the seven years I'd known him—an awareness of the emotional experience of another person. I was so moved by this glimmer of empathy that my voice cracked when I responded, which he probably mistook for upset about my uncle. He was a physicist, I said. He studied hidden symmetries, whatever those are. As I spoke, I became aware of the blue scarf around my neck. He studied weak interactions. He asked a prizewinning question about dark matter. He really loved your sister and bought two of her paintings before she blew up. Actually, he has, he had, that great portrait of you where the palmlike shapes on your shirt begin to vibrate, float away. (The grains of wood, the scalloped forms of leaves or waves, the designs in carpets, the inexact repetition of the bricks in the wall I asked you to imagine, the nectar guides in orchids—Emma's surfaces detach, but do not simply flatten or become quilt-like; the freed patterns remain in what feels like habitable space.) I remember when she painted that, he said. I don't know why I had to sit there all day since her paintings don't really look like what's in front of her. It was the summer so she was home from college and I was supposed to be doing this online high school equivalent thing. The only way she could get me to do it was by moving a TV to her studio—which was the garage, it used to be my dad's office—so I could watch while she worked. She didn't ask my mom about any of this, she just did it, and she moved a chair and a table and some other stuff to the garage so that basically she was taking apart our living room and putting it back together out there and my mom came home from work and found that she had done this and flipped out. So for a few days I sat staring at the TV and my mom kept coming over to yell at my sister and my sister would ignore her and paint. Finally my sister would kick my mom out of the garage except now the garage had become the living room and when the painting was done and we put the stuff back in the house, it didn't quite feel like the house anymore; it felt like a set. And then she just went back to college with her painting and we had to live in a house where space was reversible and sitting was posing and speech was performance and even food was a prop and so I had to bypass the time-release element by crushing and snorting and ultimately inject-ing droplets and breadcrumbs, the soft rocks between us, sealing the network of cracks in my voice, chasing the cracks as they branched. Because—no offense to your uncle—when you look into the box, the cat is supposed to be alive *or* dead, not alive *and* dead; they teach quantum superposition but expect you to function in Euclidean space, then accuse you of being distant, force you to go on these white-water rafting trips for troubled teens, try to get you to open up about your father around a firepit. There's a difference between a shaky or out-of-focus photograph and a snapshot of clouds and fog-banks. There's a difference between the twins' trajectories and I'm the earthbound one in the inertial frame that hangs in your uncle's office at MIT. Even though I was driving, writing, I shut my eyes, and they all became available to me: the venation of leaf and insect wing, the Lichtenberg figure in the grass where the discharge took place, deli-cate crazing in blue glass, the network of vessels against the black back of the lids, self-similar golden spirals, the fractals formed by river-beds and neurons, honeycomb lattices, habits, all the beautiful con-spiracies, which means "to breathe together," the ancient dream of poetry. When we arrived I double-parked and opened the trunk and he retrieved his duffel bag. Emma had texted that we were to ring the bell for the third-floor apartment and someone would come and let us in to the ground-floor apartment where her brother was going to stay, but when I rang, no one responded. I called Emma, but she didn't pick up. It was freezing and his coat didn't look warm enough and I began to worry about what would happen if I couldn't reach anyone—there was nowhere to leave him, nothing was open except for the bodega where I imagined the virus was suspended in the air like an invisible curtain of beads. I rang the bell again and texted Emma and wondered as I did so why I was the one trying to get in, trying to get in touch, and not her brother, who was almost thirty, who was just standing there in silence, who seemed strangely impervious to the weather, his affect unreadable because of the mask, but probably flat, probably quilt-like. I realized I was overfunctioning, which encouraged him to underfunction, that my care was infantilizing, and that my rising anger at Emma—why had she asked me to pick him up in the first place instead of borrowing my car and doing it herself, how could she possibly be unavailable right when he needed to be settled—indicated that a triangle was forming. (Some people, using a structure called a simplex, have tried to divide spacetime itself into tiny triangular sections, offering a theory of how the fabric of space-time evolved, how it began to flake and fall as snow.) So I decided to try to honor his competence and agency by asking him what he thought we should do, if he had any ideas about how to reach his sister or how to gain access to the apartment, but he just shrugged and produced a vape pen. Listen, I wanted to say to him, I think it might be useful if we imagine each cell in our body as a city, a city with its own bus lines, train tracks, power plants, libraries, and offices in which our portraits hang above the desks of physicists, the papers covering the desks implying they'll be right back to resume their calculations. Because—if we imagine the universe as an infinite honeycomb structure made up of such cells—some of them *will* be right back, every possibility must come to pass. But there are also patterns that migrate between cells, the branching pattern on the wallpaper in one ends up in the ice of another, and the floating signatures that cut across cells, across worlds, are, for whoever perceives them, signs of possibility. That's part of what your sister is attuning us to when she releases pattern from surface and invites us to articulate space, and I realize that this has caused you pain, that her portrait pays more attention to your T-shirt than your face. I don't think you're wrong to feel unseen. Painting is in part a defense mechanism for her: a way of looking at and looking away from simultaneously. (She's like that about your father's death. She says she's sure that the accident was basically suicide, something your mom vehemently denies, but then your sister never actually asks any questions—of the friends who were with him, police, doctors, other guests at the hotel—that would bring her any closer to the reality of what happened. We used to fight about this when we were a couple.) Abstraction is important, abstraction is necessary, otherwise we can't perceive the shapes—an ellipse, a triangle—that structure experience, provide its lattice, but she can be cold, the way the stars are cold, beautiful cold light that bends around the sun, changing the star's apparent location, a problem of measurement, prosody, the ancient dream of conspiring (the car beeped and the lights flashed twice as I unlocked it)—a dream, not a theory. But in reality, I just mumbled something about having to get home, I'm sure your sister will show up soon. When I got into the car, he slowly raised an arm; I couldn't tell if the gesture meant goodbye or wait. Now I think it meant goodbye and wait.

LES MARRONNIERS

Like a tree frequently mentioned
In the diary of an important person
A tree fighting hard in a storm
To stay literal, like character actors
Given new life in a series
The trees along the river
A common species in the temperate world
It's ok for me to walk under their flowers
It is consistent with my values to look up
The leaf scars left
On the twig, whatever that means
The flowers have an already-seen quality
I associate with objects under the sun
And I am one
Hearing "the green book stalls"
As a complete sentence
The size of a fist, the book idles
In the chest, the new-old decadence
The fast-slow time of it
The arriving early to lateness
Precocity promised me
Dusk, basically, or dusk effects
Arc lamps flicker in
The abstract sense
Of brushing up against

UNTITLED (TRIPTYCH)

It might be necessary to work backward
from toolmarks and defects in the material
on which the sky is painted, inspect the hinges
joining the sky's three panels, yet it might
also be necessary to work forward,
protecting what doesn't exist from decay
light effect by light effect. The placard says
perspective is reinvented in this picture,
those angels represent a revolution in
the depiction of angels, but the halos
don't occupy real space, all they ever wanted,
I mean the sinners on whom God has rained,
rains fire. A conservator should be prepared
to work in rain or otherwise inclement
conditions, work within an institution,
local at first, then distant, like his love,
if we're going to revolt against conventions
governing how donors are portrayed beside
angels, who mark the historical transitions.
The text says things about provenance
I can't follow, but "bequest" reminds me,
I've been meaning to bequeath an innovation,
a small innovation in a minor tradition
like this one, maybe the way I'm handling
portions of the right edge, where old light
streamed, is streaming. I'm here awaiting
test results, but know I don't get service in
medieval wings, as if the paintings stopped
time, all they wanted from their medium,

even or especially when the medium was
time, as in music. Do you know music?
Composed and performed for many purposes,
popular all over the world, in the past it was
religious, and, while I didn't know it then,
I heard some, hear it, whereas most people
alive today have only seen it. Here I am
mitering two dreams: the dream of the poem,
then the dream of the poem of that dream,
the one you write on waking, publish in
a limited edition with abundant color plates, but
you can't really join them, the dreams,
not without their collapsing into prose, so
you write two novels, waiting for results
it might be necessary to work back from.
If I got service I could hear from an office
of one sort or another, the way Rilke heard
from the torso of Apollo, only this time
it's a headless body with a bored voice
and you've returned to the Met to hide
from experience. On the backs of paintings
signs of experience are visible, conservators
date eternities. It's an everyday thing,
if you're a conservator, to restore a revelation
attributed to a disciple, then return it to storage:
the basements are full of virgins alarmed
by a sudden vision, as if Gabriel had brought
test results. And he has: You're pregnant.
But I'm a virgin! But I'm a boy! I don't

exist! Doesn't matter: they can work forward,
they can depict your crucifixion on the right
while on the left you're about to be born,
neither you nor anybody else within
the painting knows, unless you're painted
by a master, old masters can suggest
knowledge in a halo. You can't see
your own halo, it hails from the future,
scary to realize you're looking out from
a painting, that you'll crack if you blink
and yet I'm afraid that's why I'm calling.

A lot of theoretical issues surround conserving
work made out of organic substances: fat,
vegetable matter, shit and blood, dust,
toenail parings, chocolate, and the true
form of a work might be to flake, rot,
or otherwise register time, the way
I accidentally praised passages of water
damage when I visited a studio after Sandy
or the dream I had about being in the room
when the plug was pulled on Oldenburg's
Ice Bag—Scale C, a kinetic sculpture
difficult to restore, but easy to replicate,
a mode of destruction. The time is coming
when the doctor enters the room and says
we can't restore you, but here's a pamphlet
explaining replication and its pricing, or
that time has passed, I haven't kept up

since Lucía was born, and now we are
expecting another, not another Lucía,
another girl, the due date is late June,
a scheduled C for a number of reasons
Ari wouldn't want me to put in a poem
even though she knows that poems are great
places to make information disappear,
dissolve. Should it bother me that "Schedule
C" is the name of a tax form on which you list
income and expenses related to your self
employment, and is used by sole proprietors,
painters, writers? Of course it should: a curtain
divides her while they work, I can't not think
of how magicians—men—saw women
in half and yet conserve them. A fine line,
only minimal scarring, between restoring
an everyday object and making a new one,
and now many artists are designing works
they require future technology to realize,
like 4D printers, so what's conserved is virtual:
that's how I think of both poems and novels,
the main difference is in deductions, how
and how much you withhold from the actual
and for how long. Is Oldenburg dead?
Google says no, he's eighty-six at the time
of writing, but you should probably check
at the time of reading, because whether we
involve the artist, consult his intentions
is just one of the issues surrounding work

that takes up space and/or exists in time,
subject to taxation. I don't get service
in Mount Sinai, I remember from Lucía's birth,
I'll have to step back into the world to post
or receive results, funny how you can't
get calls from the institution while you're in it.
Here is a pamphlet about cord blood banking:
I can't follow what it says about provenance.

The artist desired a medium that could bind
colored particles to themselves and the support
without suppressing vibrancy as they dried,
a version of the oldest desire: to arrive
at identity through dissolution, absinthe
poured over sugar. It could have worked
for a while, but the problem is that blue,
of all the colors, is the most historical:
a blue can change its meaning in an hour
lasting years, my definition of an epoch,
not that I'll be consulted about our own
transition. Those suggestive shadows
we admired for centuries turned out to be
a consequence of candle smoke and glue
varnish, so said the restorers who developed
aggressive solvents used to remove
what they supposed were alien substances.
Now we're told the new tonal modeling
destroyed the sculptural effects we had been
right to feel dissolved by in the first place:

an expansive fold of drapery that hangs
from the lower left leg no longer sweeps
down gracefully from below the knee,
emerging abruptly at the shin instead,
a minor crime, but against humanity.
A blue that changed patterns of thinking
if not patterns of thought, for a generation
of religious scholars has obtained, is
obtaining over Brooklyn as I write this,
the first poem that mentions my daughter
by name, unless it becomes a novel.
If it does, rinse away the efflorescent salts
to reveal a poem of inaccurate vividness
I've composed without my knowledge
the way some people sleep-drive on Ambien,
America's number one prescribed hypnotic.
The blue of pills, the blue of links, the two
blue lines that indicate you're pregnant,
lapis lazuli mined in Afghanistan
then crushed to depict a donor's garment:
none of these would have appeared as blue
to the ancients, who couldn't see the color,
or so says a team of researchers at MIT
as you've probably read on the internet.
If that's true, we can't restore ancient art
without delicate optical surgeries
insurance won't cover, which means
only the wealthy will be able to afford
classical blindness. You could manage

for one, but not for two little angels, at least
not in Brooklyn, unless you move toward
genre fiction: strange to think the future
of the past depends on vampire sagas, soft
porn, first world problems, false spring
poems about death and taxes. Better to be
replicated than restored from the wrong
settings, world, or period, but it's best
to be printed layer by layer in a granular
bed, sintered by laser, or left unrealized.
Where were you when you realized the white
marble statues had once been painted
garish colors, that the Parthenon looked
like a miniature golf course in Topeka?
I was in the Roman Sculpture Court, avoiding
results among enucleated heroes, furies
a few hours ago, and thought I would
have preferred to have heard that news
from a poem, not an audio guide or placard.
Somebody should inform the eighteenth century
they are basing their revival on projected
shadows, just as someone should tell Homer
the sea is a color between violet and green
we could restore to his sight with lasers.
The problem is how to deliver the news
in a form that dissolves it into feeling
faces can be imbued with, and for conservation
purposes, the sky is the face of a period.

Today I agreed to donate all my organs
except heart valves, although it's corneas
I'd like to pass on to the future, not because
I'm so great at focusing or refracting light,
but just because I'd like to be the medium
waves enter en route to sentiment, plus
a donor poses an interesting formal challenge
since the painter must depict him both beside
the angel and a world apart, their bodies
subject to different laws, although the word
"angel" can mean donor now, confusing
exchangeability with translucence. At first
they were depicted on a smaller scale
than principal figures, compromising
linear perspective, so eventually they were
integrated into the scene, but not allowed
to touch anything, although a Madonna
might glance down benevolently at a banker
forever kneeling in the foreground. Forever
is not eternity: forever takes place in time,
whereas eternity transforms large domes
into upwardly spiraling vortices of clouds,
dissolving the ceiling, restoring it to God
who sees the future like we see the past:
painted, which must be confusing since
"the future is digital," as the poster says
at the DMV, where I don't get service, "a future
without lines." According to Wikipedia,
before the fifteenth century, a physical likeness

may not have been attempted or achieved,
only later were the donors portrayed
carefully, as historical persons instead of as
whatever the opposite of a historical person is,
an angel? Whitman? Homer? "Daughters
in particular appear as standardized beauties
in the style of the day," says no one on a page
anyone can edit or restore. She has my eyes.
We didn't name her for the patron saint
of the blind, whose remains were stolen
from Syracuse, part of why they commissioned
Caravaggio, who'd just escaped from prison,
to depict her burial, we named her for
light itself, though neither names nor light
behave that way in time. You can exchange,
the commission implies, bodies and paintings,
doing time for depicting it, suspend
sentences across lines, but you can't control
donations, your tissues could end up
supporting a face you don't believe in.
People can get paid to give sperm or eggs,
blood or plasma, but it's illegal to sell
organs, otherwise the rich would commission
the unincarcerated poor, whereas now
the rich will commission anyone, even
servants, disciples, assistants, who are often
tasked with underpainting sky, but rarely
charged with depicting impregnation
through actual light or the virtual music

we can't play in time, its instruments
still to be invented, and yet you still
hear it "in the future as in the past,"
a stillness streaming live across
margins, media. Too late to restore it and
too early, but it's always being conserved
imperfectly for the future in a poem
read forward and backward at once

inaudibly. An X-ray will discover
a hidden portrait or overturn an attribution
in my body, or the radiograph will reveal
no pentimenti, which would suggest I am
a copy, either way I'm calling now
from outside the institutions, broken
speakers beneath a weeping cherry
just off Flatbush, the cardinal's string
of down-slurred whistles, hammering in
the middle distance, police circling overhead.
That they can hover above the open-air
performance, but can't enter the invisible
theater, indicates that spring is a massive
rally against the law, the actual play
beside the point, the actors mainly kids
from the neighborhood, tinsel-wrapped
pipe cleaner halos. The youngest players
keep wandering back into history where,
swooped up by a guardian, they are restored
to the chorus, then wander off again:

I've read the polemics against the figure
of the child, agree the available futures
they are made to represent must be dissolved,
agree it's not even my place to agree,
that I largely belong to the order marked
for destruction when the revolution
in perspective is achieved, but love
I work within is not genetic, even if organic
substances are used, the smell of micro
flora blooming in the soil when it's turned,
is turning. Spring is a massive rally
creeping backward into the year, so it
gets later early now, rally against the test
results and recommended measures, serial
echoes, periodic scans. Its parapet exists
to connect the fictive world of the sacred
with the temporal one in which we view it,
more effective is how the bottom edge
of spring is burned in places: Do you sense
how the artist worked from photographs
untaken at the time, that affect here awaits
experience in form, like color in a color
word, or like a given name you less
grow into than are trained around? Yes
and no, forward and back, chain-link fence
with wine-dark blossoms I have to keep
Lucía from eating, no, they're fine to eat,
just googled it. My sorrowful expression
reveals no foreknowledge, let alone about

what's happening in a panel to my left,
the viewer's right, "he's just a donor,"
like everybody else, my features general
as money when at rest. It's raining now
it isn't, or it's raining in the near
future perfect when the poem is finished
or continuous, will have been completed
when we figure out how rain can be depicted
without a lens or window since all this
takes place when glass was rare and rain
was sometimes fire, although it's warm
enough to let her play in for a while now
it stopped. In the future there were tenses
to express what it's like to be alive today
so we won't need names, but for the present,
even though the root is war, I like Marcela,
Chela to her friends, and a friend of my
daughters' is how I think of you, reading
a poem you're on both sides of like a court
painter during a historical transition,
the restoration spring always almost is.

CONTRE-JOUR

        The light that changes
the light that goes out
when you pass under it
The unsafe intersection
and the ghost bike
The light that turns out to be a flame
and the bulb designed
to flicker. Obviously
city lights, the necklace
lights of bridges, lights of planes
are part of this, especially
        flashing or
extinguished

        Trick candle
sparking in the cake, little star
sparking, wintergreen
in the mouth, the speech of it
decaying, flash
of the muzzles as they chased
Victor Serge across the rooftops
The snow blue in the light
and the burning manuscripts
and Paris, the city of
the light that changes
        in the mouth
I wish I'd known

you were a fan of light
I would have saved some for you
Moonlight on pavement set
aside for you, in factories
in prisons, obviously
and Moscow burning obviously
in the throat I left
a light on for you, Victor Serge
in the last century, century of last
cigarettes, the light
decay gives off, the cold
       light of the living
organism

       in the open
seas, in Oakland, some
old paintings. Because like ash
it scatters, I thought that I might sing
Because it dies repeatedly
in Mexico, penniless
Penniless in Spain
I thought that I might speak
openly with you in photographs
If I appear, then obviously
I'm penniless, because appearance is
       the last resort
of light

                    Victor Serge
in his letters, in translation
Our liquidation has been prepared
and if they call your name
my hands are tied, my role is limited
to passing through
glass, to letting the glass bend
light around small corners and
translucent wings, *espejitos*
is its Spanish name, but Spain
was lost
                    Little mirrors
whose borders are

                    opaque
Can I just say one thing
about how everything is lost
one obvious thing about the threat
of sky glow and the need for dark
oases, and could Serge
be cited, traveling at a constant
speed through opaque objects like
these pages, or would that be
singing, because like ash
when you pass under it
                    because like snow
blue systems

THE CHORUS

As the only Jew in my class, it fell to me to introduce the single Ha-
nukkah song included in the annual winter concert at Randolph Ele-
mentary. All I had to do was approach the microphone and name
the preceding song (That was "Silent Night") and say what we were
singing next (Now we will present "Hanukkah, Oh Hanukkah") and
then return to my place on the metal bleachers that had been set up
in the cafeteria for the performance. I wasn't a shy kid, but this task
absolutely terrified me, and I worried about it for weeks in advance
of the concert. As soon as I knew the names of the songs in question,
I would lie awake at night practicing, repeating the words so often
their sense dissolved. Sometimes I would wake my parents up and
tell them, tears in my eyes, that I just couldn't do it, that this time I
was too frightened, and they would gently remind me that I'd said the
same thing the previous year. Benner, my dad would say, you always
do great. Benner, it's important to participate. Now a parent myself, I
assume they discussed whether they should talk to my teachers and
relieve me of this burden or whether I needed to face my fears, gain
experience. I'm not criticizing them, but it's horrible to separate from
a chorus, to address a crowd of elders, and then return to the group
and sing, although really I just mouthed the words, afraid my voice
would be conspicuous. There is always a gap between songs, tradi-
tions, and a child must bridge it (or there will be violence) and that's
what the songs themselves tell us if we listen. I love the popular song
where the singer talks about how her tears are hidden by the rain,
the song of the individual and collective, lyric and epic, and I'd like
to sing it for you now, but I can't, all I can do is introduce it, reintro-
duce it like a threatened species into the alders, the poplars between
us. That was "The Little Drummer Boy" and this is sense behaving
like a liquid, assuming the shape of its container. My Little League

pitching coach, Bob Lolly, is the one who first called me Benner. The league was incredibly competitive, overserious. Did a nine-year-old really need a dedicated pitching coach, home and away uniforms, fitted caps embroidered with our initials? (Bob Lolly was a powerful figure for me because he always claimed that he could teach me an unhittable curveball, but that he wouldn't, because it would damage my developing arm and ruin my long-term athletic prospects.) Our games were rituals in which sons were reduced to tears by fathers: when a kid struck out, a father, often beer-drunk, would tell him to get his head out of his ass, to get in the fucking game, to keep his eye on the ball, etc., and the son would return to the dugout in shame, sit apart from his teammates and cry, rivulets forming in his eye-black. But not me: my dad would applaud no matter what, even if I struck out swinging wildly at a pitch in the dirt: Great swing, Benner, you'll hit it next time! I love you! I'm not criticizing him, but these expressions of support humiliated me, marked me as different. The worst experience of my time in Little League, what more or less ended it, was when all my dad's siblings flew in from the coasts for my older brother's Bar Mitzvah and attended, over my objections, a game where I was pitching. Despite Bob Lolly's guidance and exhortations, I could not throw a strike. And yet every pitch I threw resulted in wild applause from my people in the bleachers, rattling me more and more, until I was walking in runs, hitting batters, but Lolly wouldn't pull me from the game, given that my family was visiting from far away, even though we needed the win for our rankings, even though my teammates and their parents in the stands were seething. Finally, he called a time-out and jogged out to the mound and said to me: Benner, I am going the way of the earth and you should strengthen yourself and become a man. The way the Torah is to be sung is inseparable from its sense, that's why proper cantillation was taught to Moses with the vowels, although some of the original tune has been lost, there's a gap now—a gap in song is called a rain delay—and you must inhabit it, let your body be the bridge. My daughters, ages five and seven, recently noticed my parents calling me Benner when we were in Sanibel and they found it hilarious. At first my kids only called me Benner as a joke, would say it and crack up, but soon it became a habit and they'd say it without trying to be funny. Benner, can I have a snack. Benner, I had a nightmare, will you stay with me for a while. Benner, where is Mommy. My children aren't really Jewish—their mother is a nonpracticing Catholic—but we celebrate Hanukkah, we sing Hanukkah songs together, although I often have to make up the lyrics. For some reason I cannot remember words set to music, a fact that has always troubled me, since most people experience music as mnemonic. If I want to learn a song, I have to learn it in two parts, on two tracks, committing the words to memory first and then the melody, which is why I don't know any songs to speak of, why I'm always speaking of song instead of singing, and how I've come to introduce false songs to my children; one day they will discover that the lyrics aren't timeworn, haven't circulated. That was "Joy to the World" and this is a Torah portion about parallel mirrors sung in the perfect pitch our fathers withheld from us, not because they didn't want us to have it, but because they didn't think we could handle it, they feared it would ruin the long-term prospects of our voices, that it would be better for us to discover the secret on our own—or not discover it, not discovering it is fine, too, Benner, it's really up to you. If you are feeling so crummy about the concert that you want us to ask Mr. Holloman to make another arrangement, we will. We hear you that you're upset and we're willing to do that and we're sure he'd understand. But it's late—we can't call him now—and you might feel differently in the morning. What I've learned is that the hardest part of the winter concert for you is the worry itself—that once you get up there on the stage you do a great job and you have a good feeling afterward. But like I say it's up to you. When I was a kid, my dad was way too intense about this kind of thing. There used to be an annual school musical in which everybody had to participate and even though I'd always get a tiny role, often not even a speaking part, just kind of had to skip around stage in a costume, I'd get really nervous. I wouldn't have ever thought to share that anxiety with my dad who would have given me some speech about representing the family, honoring the family, being a man, getting in the game, which for him meant withholding. For him, for Grandpa, withholding was the task that falls to each generation like rain, like tears (rhymes with "cares") in rain through which the sense escapes, you have to catch it on your tongue, you have to participate, that's what his father had always said to him. But I understand that—while the introduction just takes a few seconds to deliver, while Hanukkah isn't even a major holiday—the worry can last ten thousand years, that's the miracle. Your mom and I are fine with whatever you choose, we'll be proud of you either way. But you do have to choose.

ALSO KNOWN AS HURTSICKLE, CYANI FLOWER, AND BACHELOR'S BUTTON

Light snow falling in the listening
area, something has to keep me from
the radio and other forms of incidental
contact like *The current time is*
or *I see silver plunging in the days ahead.*
Why not poetry? AM clouds give way
to PM sun. I wish I'd written that
and did, and publish it on air
the way a match publishes in my hand

before I hold it to the cigarette I took
from my first teacher's son in light
snow at her improvised wake, contract
pneumonia there, let it bloom
in the left lung for a while, then postpone
Berlin. *I discourage you from flying*
is the nicest thing anyone has ever
except maybe the command to *look*
alive when I was a boy undead among

small purple flowers in the outfield.
The plan was to wander around Kreuzberg
mourning, but this will do: overheard
forecasts, adjustments to internal
flora, light snow that turns to rain in time,
just not *for* anything. If you turn
literally inward, touch the breastbone

with radiation, locate a shadow, then
the tech will print you out an image, freeing

up the elegy for other things, like wandering
beyond the field of play while bases
empty. (They're talking about *the off-season*,
beautiful phrase that's mine and now
it's gone.) Cornflower, bluebottle,
the involucre is urn-shaped and the margins
irregularly cleft. Thrives on roadsides,
thrives on waste sites, is sometimes
toothed or lobed.

I think you need either meaning or a sense that it has fled, especially when you look up. You need rudimentary fastening devices, something that binds surfaces, that resists, however ineffectually, their separation. Tar from the dry distillation of birch bark, a piece of music to coordinate work. I personally need cities at night, stars occluded but inferred, abandoned financial districts, underground tunnels where gold is moved back and forth between vaults. I like to imagine that's my job, that I stack gold on pallets underneath Manhattan and transport them short distances with a forklift, that I literalize the day's trades, that I have a career in "gold custody." A world needs gold bars moving underground, although they cannot be pure; if they were pure they'd be too malleable to hold their shape over time and so each bar contains a small amount of other metals—copper, iron, silver, platinum, which gives the gold a whitish shade. Shades and impurities that let us hold our shapes are minimum conditions for a world, but many worlds are brief, a pulse moving through a medium, many worlds collide and recombine as you walk through them, which feels like a succession of webs on the face: *plash, plash, plash*, but without sound. We need music without sound to coordinate the work of moving through minimal worlds of alders, hazels, hornbeams—trees that rapidly colonize open ground after a fire. I have this dream in which I walk across the bridge after the fire to find downtown covered in even stands of birch with peeling, papery bark on which the names of everyone who has ever lived are written phonetically and I look down to find the pavement is clear glass and the gold is moving underground and I look up at the sky to watch the meaning flee, the patterned flight of meaning; I assume everyone has a version of this dream, but forgets it upon waking. We, at least my friends and I, often describe ourselves as *moved* by music, at the height of feeling we acknowledge that we are objects passed from one place to another, soft metal, and I think those are the minimal conditions of person-hood, necessary but insufficient: we must be storable, impure, capable of movement. Once I was coming back on the Amtrak from Boston with John. He was a mess and I was basically dragging him back to the city so I could watch him, so you and I could take turns watching him, his fretted neck and hollow body, a gentle custody. We were sit-ting behind two young women—maybe college students—who were discussing a passage in Dostoyevsky, in which the prisoners in Siberia wanted to put on a play for Christmas. Together they made a curtain out of "pieces of linen, old and new, given by the convicts; shirts, the bandages which our peasants wrap around their feet in lieu of socks, all sewn together well or ill, and forming together an immense sheet. Where there was not enough linen, it had been replaced by writing paper, taken sheet by sheet from the various office bureaus." Listening to these kids discuss this passage in whispers as John pressed his face into my neck, as we crawled across the Northeast Corridor in winter, industrial ruins in moonlight through the window—it grew acutely beautiful in their paraphrase, how the prisoners painted the curtain black, painted it with stars, hung it from the ceiling, dividing worlds, defeating time, suspending labor. *See*, I kept whispering to John, *see*, *see*. Later, in Penn Station, after we'd taken the escalator up to the main level, we again found ourselves beside the two young readers on the platform for the downtown A. I wanted to say something to them, to thank them, but I didn't know how. Then John reached into the duffel bag and removed three heavy bars, held them out to me. One was rectangular with rounded sides, indicating it was from the Denver Assay Office; one had square edges, which meant it was cast in New York before 1986; the third conformed to the trapezoidal shape characteristic of the contemporary international standard and had a greenish hue (iron). I tapped one of the women on the shoulder and said, although not in these words, *plash, plash, plash.* Only then did we hear one busker's violin, another's balalaika. A bar for him, for the rats scavenging between the rails, see the gold devour them, and a bar for young men dancing on the train, a hymn to possibility, a few bars of the underground malleable music my friends and I distribute. When we were back on open ground, walking along DeKalb, it began to rain, John began to lose his shape, I didn't know if we'd reach my apartment in time, let alone in space. When we were nearing the park, these two kids with shaved heads stopped us, blocked our progress when we said excuse me, tried to pass. One of them leaned in and said: Give us your fucking money. And the other kid raised his sweatshirt to show the handle of a gun tucked in his waistband. Give us your fucking money now. But we don't have any money, I said, as calmly as possible, which was true. Please, I said, we just have this heavy bag of gold bars, which are stamped, which aren't fungible, cannot circulate. At that point I noticed the bandages around their feet. At that point I realized these two boys were girls, they were the two girls who had been talking about Dostoyevsky on the train. They must have followed us, they must have been following us our whole lives, forgotten upon waking. Their disguises fell away, their skin began to glow, the rain stopped, the rain seemed to hang against the hammered background of the sky. And they said, although not in words, we have come to relieve him of his duffel, to end one world so you can start another. Because a world ends every few seconds and must be rebuilt, worlds end and are rebuilt, a rocking motion. I think what's hard for me, John said when we were back at my apartment processing the experience, sitting in the window smoking those tiny

British cigarettes he always carried, I think what's hard for me is the feeling that I'm totally without bourgeois respectability—I lost yet another job, Cora and I have broken up, for real this time, over the kid question, I'm certainly no comfort to my parents—but I also have no access to the value or intensities of art, mine or anybody else's, highs that might make the lows in some sense worth it. We both know my recent sound installations are bullshit. And this sense of being a burden on my friends, on you and Ben in particular. And this sense of the irrelevance of it all given the political situation. And then—Stop, I interrupted, just stop for a second, John, and listen. Listen to the wind in the birches, a stream of alephs, the room tone of the forest, sirens in the distance, folk music, unnecessary but sufficient. I personally need cities at night, clear glass pavement, impurities, writing paper, all forming together an immense patchwork curtain. I'm listening now, John, Jack, Josh, Josiah, James. Tell me what you need.

ROTATION

1

I was going to praise the transpersonality of print over the
    individuality of handwriting
I was going to praise the viewer constructed by monochromy
I was going to describe the remarkable comeback intention is
    making in new music and praise that
Desire for accessibility flaring up inside me as I praise the fantasy of
    corporate personhood

In the brief window between takeoff and the use of approved
    electronic devices I believe great change is possible
I believe it while banking hard to the east to find smoother air
When I can't tell if a person is joking I believe in the power of poetic
    modality, to hear this *as* music,
to see this *as* an experiment in the collectivization of feeling, no
    matter if failed

Red glow of the clock tower visible from our window and red glow
    of the alarm clock beside the window
collaborate on a claim about color and synchrony until the former
    loses minutes in high wind
Then the claim devolves into a sigh acknowledging the futility of
    administration, a fallacy
I praise for its mutability and enlist

2

I cannot express in the language of logical entailment my love for
    you, the second person plural
on the perennial verge of existence, like color almost becoming
    surface
I reach for a verb that isn't there but experience its shape, then
    back-form a phantom subject
with whom I identify, walking through the park at night

There is nothing more beautiful than a vulnerable grid
glowing in late empire, which is how I think of you, streetlights
    flickering
I think of you as a friend who continues to speak to me, not
    realizing the call was dropped, or as
my denied freedom returning in the form of atonality

not when breaking glass wakes me, but when it enters the dream as
    orchestral innovation
I guess I'm waiting for you to read this back to me in a voice I can
    entrain into the actual, tiny wings
brushing the lips, beginning to make sense, oceanic
tone suspended undecidably between exuberance and flatness

3

I have almost none of the characteristics of the well-made man Walt
Whitman enumerates
All I have is a kind of supersensitivity to harbor lights and skylines,
which come at me hard
It's like smoking with the patch on for me to be in time, like waving
to someone
who was waving to someone behind me for us to correspond

But we do correspond, like a crisis in easel painting and a dirty war
Soft glow of the Kindle when the train enters a tunnel, I would
probably reach more readers
if I went on tour, but I'm dead and busy with teaching
I'm standing before a kind of allover abstraction the placard says I'm
part of,

unprimed ground returning as figure, figure coming at me hard
I carry its afterimage into the park and lay it down like a lily where a
falling branch struck a child
While I wait to be reanimated briefly by an as yet only hypothesized
force,
I keep my practice virtual

4

And there *are* real forces at work in the popular, I acknowledge that
    now, I am seeking out forms
of acknowledgment, this is one, let me know if it counts for you,
    brother
That's a great word, like "bread" or "death," let's add it to the list of
    things to recover for the noncommercial
floating city I'm building out of trash and hair, the car alarms that
    follow thunder,

out of rain and thunder and bread and sex, this is a model, not sure
    if it scales
Like Sei Shōnagon, I am making a list of things that quicken the
    heart, and you can be on it
I am having a frank conversation regarding the permissibility of
    violence during the long transition
to reenchantment, and you can leave comments

Out of the bright, perpetual midnight of the truck stop, I saw a man
    emerge barefoot
Out of the empirical fact of contingency I saw a relation of great
    delicacy grow, trellis and vine
and thunder and work, I acknowledge that now
I acknowledge that dark and light as modeling tools must cede to
    warm and cool

5

I just learned their screens don't glow, they depend, like moons, on
   an external light source
I had known, but forgotten, that the moon is slowing the Earth's
   rotation, minutely lengthening the day
Learning some facts feels like remembering, as they fit into a place
   other facts have prepared for them
We can carry the shape of a fact we don't know around like a
   photograph

of a missing loved one, though any isolated fact is useless
The steady stream of isolated facts we call information distracts us
   from a basic fact whose shape we carry
This shape has a volume and we try to fill it with colloids, smoke
   and foam
When we encounter this missing fact, we will for the first time
   experience integrity, which will feel

like remembering, reemerging from a tunnel into rain, I know
I read somewhere in the dark that a transpersonal subject capable of
   ending the permanent war
is the still unconstituted whole, the poem
its figure in slow rotation, and each of us carries a volume

6

This is the short transitional phase between organic imagery and a
    mature vocabulary
of great rectilinear severity, the sun gone cadmium among ambient
    particulates
This is the brief window in which the beautiful etymologies return,
    when you can intuit a future usage
in a slur, vinho verde on the roof, skeletonized foliage where we saw
    those iridescent beetles mate

A kind of mock vampirism is spreading fast among America's teens
    and we must support it,
their desire to be marked and live forever, their refusal to reflect, salt
    on the neck maybe the best salt there is
I am willing to stand with any experimental form of sociality
    grounded in twilight, and it is a ground
You can sift a handful, see flakes of mica sparkle

in the moment before the acrylic dries, before it's recuperated into
    the white walls of medium specificity
Because of expanding underwater plumes, a desperate pluralism has
    obtained, and you can say anything
in loose hexameters, help me gather these
quickly, before the night work on the bridge begins

THE ROSE

1

It is a clichéd dream, she said, a common
I used to think libraries were quiet because
the way they ban flash photography
books were corroded by speech, the pigments
The one where it's night in the institution
A corduroy bear hides from the watchman
The animals speak at the zoo and sculptures
Relax, stretch, walk around the atrium
low voices to protect the blue glass in the
Supply chain problems, how the mica sparkles
in Jay DeFeo's *The Rose*, which I saw first
with Margaux when the new Whitney opened, then
When I was sleeping, the mica sparkling in red
security light, and in my dreams all light is
The way you are everyone in the dream
heat, she lit a cigarette off the screen
blue embers. Like those Magritte paintings where
the house is illuminated by a streetlamp but
a daytime sky, I mean it's like that to be alive
and made of cloth, and writing this down

In the notebook she keeps by the bed, there are
There is a small light coming up the escalator
I like the poem your son wrote about the wolf
that it has needs, that its first need is meat
spelled "met," and the second the moon
That the moon is a need that can be met
in the city, whereas the stars are obscured
is cliché, a commons, because they also dream

the institutions, that's why I like teaching at night
how *The Rose*, too expensive to restore
too heavy to move, was for years behind a false
wall in San Francisco, and the seminars
on art took place in its presence, invisible
Walls have an unconscious, needs
sleep and oxygen, a pack and large silver fish
spelled "pac," and my friends and I walk through it
at night, to see what has shifted beneath
the sawtooth skylights, on the soft grass
the little stars, we are tucked in
to the walls around the fire. I'd like to begin

2

I'd like to begin tonight, he said, by telling you two stories about the power of institutions. When I was eight, the age Lucía is now, my mom's friend Shirley took me and my brother to a sleepover in the Seattle Aquarium's famous "undersea glass dome." Before they turned the lights out, a woman made a series of announcements, emphasizing, among other things, that food of any sort was prohibited. We had sleeping bags and I had my *Star Wars* pillow. Sharks and rays floated through the watery heavens above us. At some point, Shirley whispered that she'd brought us a treat, and she showed us two small bags of those sugar-coated gummy orange slice candies, which we loved. They seemed to glow in the dark. My brother was thrilled, but I was horrified, maybe because I was so rarely away from my parents at night that I couldn't tolerate any sign of unpredictability in my guardian. Or maybe I thought the ban on eating was crucial for our safety, that if the sharks or rockfish somehow sensed the candies, they'd come after them, slamming their cold smooth bodies again and again into the glass until it cracked and four hundred thousand gallons of water came crashing down upon us. It must have shocked Shirley when I started to cry, to panic, repeating no, no, no, as she held the small bag toward me, the other "campers" turning small flashlights in our direction. Eventually they calmed me down, Shirley putting both bags of candy back into her purse, infuriating my brother. I remember a sleepless night, trying to keep the dome intact with the pressure of my gaze, though I probably slept for hours. Later that year (this is the second story), I overheard my parents discussing their concerns about my going on the Cub Scouts camping trip because I had recently started walking in my sleep. (I could hear my parents through their wall if I went into my bedroom's closet.) My mom was afraid that I would leave the tent and walk off a cliff or into a lake and my dad kept saying that he understood her concern, but they couldn't make all their parenting decisions out of fear, I needed to have experiences; they could talk to Dana, the "den mother," to plead for extra vigilance. I had no desire to go camping, at least not without my parents, to have to hold up the dome of the sky, so I started pretending to sleepwalk more aggressively with the goal of scaring my parents into keeping me home. When I actually sleepwalked, I had always stayed on the same floor as our bedrooms, usually going into my parents' room and speaking in tongues before calmly going back to bed, but now I made a point of walking noisily downstairs, opening and shutting the front door, although I never left the house. One night when I was banging around in the kitchen, my exhausted dad came downstairs to get me, to coax me gently back to bed, but this time he himself appeared to be more asleep than awake, his eyes half-shut; he was mumbling incomprehensibly. The panic again: I'm awake, Dad, I'm awake, I said, desperate to rouse him. I have only been pretending to sleepwalk. Because I don't want to have experience.

3

For the next seven years she applied thick paint
chiseled it away, inserting wooden dowels
of the gaze to support the thick impasto
which shifted overnight, transferring it with friends
The way they warn you that articles
may have shifted during flight, it applies to sleep
Wedged out of a bay window on Fillmore Street
after we sawed through the frame, it reminds me of
All my favorite books were about built spaces
shading into wilds, worlds, Narnia through the wardrobe
The prince they tied to a chair, who said
No matter what I say, don't untie me, stop your ears
Max's bedroom becoming jungle, Harold drawing the moon
into existence, inadvertently making the sea
when his hand trembled, and the number seven
I read them to my girls, Marcela puts a book
under the pillow to "help me dream," the door opens onto
forest, because you know the people who built it
are in your walls, that your needs have been met
at the expense of other wolves

is part of Margaux's work. We saw it get restored
restore itself before our eyes, and like a star collapse
inward continuously before us, saw
through the frame, and I said the rose is obsolete
quoting, renews itself in metal or porcelain so that
I was splicing lines, to engage roses
becomes a geometry, end quote, and the guard
said to her, No flashes, when she didn't have

She wasn't holding anything, is the nicest
thing anyone has ever said to me
In a dream, you are everyone, even the walls
You sleepwalk through your seminar on modernist
low voices, you aren't supposed to wake them
your parents, just gently suggest that they return
So I can relax about influence in her presence
I make a list of my needs: light and heat
"met" and fish, a pact to hold the dome
up above the world so high, like a diamond
and a notebook, a supply chain of our own making
Oxygen, clean water, libraries, caves

This song is dedicated, this song goes out, is for. I wrote it in a dream, the second-oldest song in the world. It's about hours without wages, blue hours, and the lyrics are loosely based; the lyrics recall. They're anonymous and attributed like rain. I want everybody out there to sing along, even the stones. I want all the lovely people laboring in the dark. Wind in the poplars, overheard speech, traffic noise, receding sirens, people picking glass from the recycling, the whistle and report of illegal fireworks, the report of gunshots, laughter through a wall, the laughter of children—these are my people, swaying imperceptibly. You know all the words because there aren't any, but there is an addressee, you are the implied recipient of the words in the song from and for the future I recorded on my phone in a common dream, for dreams are commons. The screen is badly cracked and I get glass in my finger every time I touch it. Something is lost in the transcription because it doesn't have words, but room tone is gained, a sound bed is made. That's why I'm sending my friends links: I want my friends linked and listening as they fan out across the bridges until it is part of the folk tradition, the blue tradition, the wordless silent part I anonymously contributed by living. Paintings sing it at night, an exhalation, even though all of those words are wrong. The song goes on forever then it stops. Its basic idea is that time can be defeated for an hour if everyone breathes together, but songs are not made out of ideas, they're made out of glass, the aerosolized glass that shows up in the lungs. Here is the chorus of the song: the instant before music. It's a little sentimental, the poem that describes the song that would be general. Like my daughters, sentimental, irresponsible, and strong; like my sons: irascible, unborn. This song goes out like a candle in the wind. My dad says he named me after "Bennie and the Jets"; in reality, I was named after my great-grandfather on my mother's side, but my dad sang it to me in Stormont Vail. My belief is that the first experience of language comes from the father and is sung, sentimental, popular, that song is populated, that even I am dedicated and go out. If you see the *i* as a candle, if *i*'s are dotted with flame and flicker, then a song has entered circulation. And if I were holding a son in a hospital blanket now, if his face were bruised and purple beneath his cap, if I were singing to that son while looking out through the window onto the park, he would be my princess, all of the popular songs would be about him, hang about him like a mist. All I need my song to one day say is you are my princess and my father and you're breathing glass, soft glass that links you, that rain outside of time is mist, is glass, and I want you to fan out and take the bridges.

NO ART

Tonight I can't remember why
everything is permitted or,
what amounts to the same thing,
forbidden. No art is total, even

theirs, even though it raises
towers or kills from the air,
there's too much piety in despair
as if the silver leaves behind

the glass were politics
and the wind they move in
and the chance of scattered
storms. Those are still

my ways of making and
I know that I can call on you
until you're real enough
to turn from. Maybe I have fallen

behind, am falling, but
I think of myself as having
people, a small people
in a failed state, and love

more avant-garde than shame
or the easy distances.
All my people are with me now
the way the light is.

ACKNOWLEDGMENTS

Grateful acknowledgment is made to the following publications, in which these poems first appeared, often in different versions: *Bomb, Brick, Frieze, Granta, Harper's Magazine, Lana Turner, London Review of Books, The New Yorker, The New York Review of Books,* and *The Paris Review.* "The Dark Threw Patches Down upon Me Also" was made into a chapbook by students at the Center for Book and Paper Arts at Columbia College. "Untitled (Triptych)" was printed in a limited edition with monotypes by Wendy Mark. Several of the prose poems were included in *Gold Custody,* a collaboration with Barbara Bloom, published by Mack Books.

"Contre-Jour" is in memory of John Berger. "Also Known as Hurtsickle . . ." is in memory of C. D. Wright. *Omnia quae sunt, lumina sunt.*

A NOTE ABOUT THE AUTHOR

Ben Lerner is the author of seven previous books of poetry and prose, as well as several collaborations with visual artists. The recipient of fellowships from the Fulbright, Guggenheim, and MacArthur Foundations, Lerner has been a finalist for the National Book Award for Poetry and the Pulitzer Prize for Fiction, among many other honors. He is a Distinguished Professor of English at Brooklyn College.